Clara Morris

A Silent Singer

Clara Morris

A Silent Singer

ISBN/EAN: 9783743305694

Manufactured in Europe, USA, Canada, Australia, Japa

Cover: Foto ©ninafisch / pixelio.de

Manufactured and distributed by brebook publishing software (www.brebook.com)

Clara Morris

A Silent Singer

Contents

	PAGE
A Silent Singer	1
An Old Hulk	35
The Gentleman Who Was Going To Die	71
Old Myra's Waiting	93
"In Paris, Suddenly———"	161
Two Buds	173
The Ambition of MacIlhenny	197
John Hickey: Coachman	217
Black Watch	241
Dinah	257
Life's Aftermath	293

A Silent Singer

It had been a hot day, and the minister had brought us, my mother and myself, from the city to his country home, in a mysterious, antediluvian species of buggy. Of all the race of men it is the country minister alone who can discover this particular breed of buggy. They are always gifted with strange powers of endurance; never being purchased until they have seemingly reached the point of dissolution, they will thereafter, for years and years, shake and totter, and rattle and rock, carrying all the time not only people but almost every conceivable kind of merchandise, from a few pounds of groceries to a pumpkin or a very youthful calf, without coming one step nearer their final wreck.

This special buggy could hold one person in comfort, two in discomfort and three in torture. I had been the party of the *third* part in that day's ride, and worn out and crumpled and dusty, we passed from darkness into a room full of lamp-light and faces. I was trying to support myself steadily upon a pair of legs so recently aroused from dumb sleep that they had barely reached the ticklish stage, and the ten thousand needle-prickling power was in full blast when the Rev. Hyler introduced me to his seven sons. My dazzled eyes and tired mind made them seem full seventeen to me, and they were so big and rough and noisy, I hung my head, confused, disappointed, frightened even, and then I felt the gentle pressure of her hot little hand on mine.

I raised my childish eyes and saw the sweetness of the smile upon her pallid face, saw it dawn upon her lips, pass swiftly to the dimple in her cheek, hide a moment there, only to reappear the next dancing in the sapphire blueness of her eyes—saw and mentally bowed down and worshipped her from that moment. Physically, I clung close to her burning hand and gave her back a smile of such astounding breadth and frankness as must have revealed to her my entire dental economy; and when, a few minutes later, I learned that she whispered because her voice was gone—lost forever, I felt such a passion of love and pity for her, such a longing to spare her suffering, that, but for its absurdity, I could have wounded my own flesh that I might bear the pain in her name. Grown-ups do not always understand the strength of feeling young things are capable of.

Next day we two round pegs began fitting ourselves into the new holes prepared for us, and though they were not absolutely square, they were still far enough from roundness to be very uncomfortable holes indeed. My mother began her never-ending duties of housekeeper. Mrs. Hyler had broken down from overwork and sick-nursing, and I having, as my mother once declared, " as many eyes as had a peacock's tail," began my almost unconscious observations of a new form of poverty. (I already had a really exhaustive knowledge of the subject both from observation and from personal experience, and I had come to the conclusion that the bitterness of poverty was greatly influenced by the manner in which it was accepted. I had known abject, ragged poverty to enjoy streaks of real merriment on comparatively comfortable occasions, while higher up in life those who openly acknowledged their poverty seemed only to suffer its inconvenience and to know nothing of the shame and humiliation of those who tried to hide theirs by agonizing makeshifts.) Here I found it was accepted in sullen silence, but, nevertheless, bitter resentment lowered on every face save my dear Miss Linda's.

She always turned to those eighteen watchful, loving eyes a sweetly-smiling, pallid face with serene brows; but I saw her sometimes when smile and serenity were both gone and her face was anguished.

The Rev. Hyler, minister, farmer, father of seven sons, was himself a seventh son, and had he been examined at his birth with that closeness of scrutiny given to first-born babies, I'm positive the word "failure" could have been found plainly stamped upon his small person. He was a tall, gray, narrow man, and seemed always to have a bitter taste in his mouth. Black-coated, white-tied and pale, he seemed to have been pressed between the leaves of some old volume of sermons and left there till all the color and sap had dried out of him as it might dry out of a pressed violet or pansy. Perpetual ill-humor had stamped to the very bone the three-lined frown he wore between his eyebrows. He was an educated man and full of information—that was of no use to him. He could give statistics as to the number of the inhabitants of Palestine, but he could not tell whether an unsatisfactory field required topdressing or under-draining. He had been an instructor, a teacher; had, in fact, been at the head of one of the State colleges, but failed and came back, much embittered, to the small church he had left with such high hopes; but finding he had provided himself with more mouths than his salary could well fill he had taken to farming, at which he seemed to be the greatest failure of all.

Narrow and cold by nature, soured by disappointment, he loved but one person on earth, and that person was his first-born child, his only daughter, Linda. He admired her, he was proud of her, he loved her, truly and tenderly, beyond a doubt; but, alas, as surely beyond a doubt, his was a jealous and a selfish love, and she, with eyes whose power and penetration fully equalled their rare beauty of coloring, read him through and through, as she might have read a book! Saw the dry, gray man's weakness of resolve, his bitter temper, his small tyrannies, and worse—far worse, because that was a most repellant sin—his hypocrisy; saw all these things and with no touch of sympathy for any one of them, but, with what seemed almost divine compassion, she gave him reverent service and such tender, loyal love as many a better father fails all his life to win.

And this sweet Linda, woman-grown—this young lady who had "come out," and had had a season of social gaiety in the city—who—oh, wondrous being! had had real "for true" lovers—she stooped from her high estate to honor me with her attention, her conversation—even, to a certain point, her confidence—while I had only reached that humiliating stage in life where old ladies could refer to me as a "growing girl." And this condescension filled me with such joy—such stupendous pride—I marvel it did not precede a mighty fall. But, looking back upon it all, I think I see a pathetic reason for that unequal companionship. My mother, knowing me to be painfully sensitive to suffering or sorrow, kept from me the knowledge that the girl I so loved was slowly dying, a victim of that fell disease, consumption! Her days were so surely numbered that no one had the faintest hope that she would see the yellowing of the leaves that now danced greenly on the trees. I saw her pale and very, very fragile, and only loved her more. I saw her faint sometimes, but I had seen other women faint when I knew they were not ill, and, to my childish ideas, any one who rose from her bed and dressed each day must surely be quite well. So it came about that in my eyes alone she belonged still to the world of the living—in my face alone could she read love without anxiety, and when she laughed, as she often did, it was only in my eye she found a hearty, gay response, for every other glance was full of anguished pity.

If my ignorance was not bliss, it was, at least, I truly think, a comfort to her, since by its help she could forget for a time, at least, that she was doomed and set aside as having nothing more to do with life. And my profound interest and *naïf* admiration egged her on to tell me of the gay, sweet past—such an innocent, pitifully short past it was—of her small triumphs and her pretty frocks. Sometimes she would even show me her few girlish trinkets, but I was quick to observe that if I ever asked about her future use of them a sort of shudder passed over her white face and her eyes would close quickly for a moment; then she would answer evasively, gently; yet there was a flatness in the tones of her voice, and she would surely remark, "that she would try now to doze a little."

It was not long before my observation brought me closer to her tender heart, while slowly I learned, little by little, something of the weight of the cross this fragile girl was bearing on her trembling shoulders.

Mrs. Hyler was, I think, the most disconcerting person in this uncomfortable family. Her manner toward them was that of a moderately devoted housekeeper—head nurse, who presumed slightly by reason of her long service. The last scant drop of kindness—the last ray of warmth of affection—I dare not use a stronger word—was for her Linda! But we must remember that for four and twenty years she had listened to what the Rev. Hyler " was going to do," and had suffered from what the Rev. Hyler "did not do," and there was no hope left in her.

I shall not introduce her sons individually, but will simply state that between the Spanish-looking eldest one—brave, loyal, honest and kind—and the impish youngest, with the face of a blond seraph and a heart like a nether mill-stone, there were five others, each one striving to be—or so it seemed—as unlike his brothers as possible. In all their lives they had found but two subjects they could agree upon; on these, however, they were as one boy. Their honest, hearty love for "Sister Linda" was one subject, and a fixed determination to "get even" with their father was the other.

Linda Hyler loved music profoundly, and she had not only natural talent, but powers of concentration and a capacity for hard work that might have made an artist of her. And the poor child had had her opportunity—for one with means and power and the inclination to use them, attracted by the purity and volume of her voice and by her earnest ambition, had offered to assist her to that stern training, so difficult in those days to obtain, even when one had the money to pay for it. But if she had talent, she also had a father, and he with the bitter-taste seemingly strong in his mouth, refused the kindly offer, giving no nobler reason for his act than that "she was his only daughter and he would miss her far too much." She pleaded with him in vain, and had the pain of seeing her one opportunity float away from her, taking on, as it went, all the airy grace, all the glancing beauty of a bubble floating in the sunshine.

Had her father not provided so much material for its building, the cross she bore might not have been so heavy. Up to the time of our arrival, Linda had managed to sit a little while each day before the battered old organ that stood in an otherwise empty room. To any other family it would have been the parlor—to this family it was a thing without a name. But even as you have seen a timid, lonely woman appear at her window, whistling loudly and wearing a man's hat —by means of which she convinces would-be burglars of the presence there of a large and very destructive man—so these parlor windows were well curtained, that the occasional humped-over, slow-driving passer-by might be convinced that this parlor held—(as much ingrain-horse-hair-worsted-crocheting, and high art plaster cats, with round black spots and heavy coats of varnish as any)—and I suppose that one trick was quite as convincing as the other—any way, there sat Linda in that dreary room, before the organ, drawing from its sulky and unwilling interior sounds of such solemn sweetness as made one pray involuntarily; and sometimes she played simply an accompaniment—sitting with lifted face and closed eyes, the veins swelling in her throat, but no sound coming from her moving lips. Already I had become her second shadow, and so I'd creep into the empty room after her, and listen to her playing, and once when I was greatly moved, she turned to me and said: "Little Sister"—the pet name she had graciously bestowed on me—"what does that make you think of?"

And without a pause I answered eagerly: "A church—not," I hurriedly explained, "not our church, but a great one with pictures, and lots of people, and lights and sweet-smoke!"

Ah, how she laughed, and though it was but a husky whispering affair, it was still a very merry laugh, because of the light that danced so gaily to it in her eyes. She then informed me that the music had been a mere scrap from a famous oratorio, and that my "sweet-smoke" was called incense, and though she set me right, it was her harmless jest to use the word "sweet-smoke" herself ever after.

We had been there but a little while, when one day I noticed something wrong with the music; the tones were weak and wavering, there seemed to be no certainty in her touch. Her little hand could not hold a simple chord with firmness, and then the next moment there was a soft crash of the yellow, old keys, as Linda sank forward helpless and panting. I sprang to help her, and between two struggling, unwilling breaths, I heard her whisper: "Must this go too? Dear God! must this go too?"

By chance the little brother had been present. He called his mother, and presently Linda was on the sofa in the other room, and the inevitable farm-house remedy for all mortal ills, the camphor-bottle—or to use the rural term, the "camfire"—had been produced, and soon Linda raised her eyes and called up the old, sweet smile; while little Arthur stood with sturdy legs far apart—his hands in his small pockets, and his father's own special brand of frown upon his brow—watching his sister's restoration; then he remarked: "Linda, it was blowin' wind into that d——blamed old organ, that busted yer all up just now!—so it was!—and after this yer just pull yer feet back out of the way, and I'll crawl under there, and work them 'pedal treadle things,' and blow yer all the wind yer want—and if I blow so hard it busts the thing, papa darsent lick me, 'cause I'll be doin' it for you!" and he danced with malicious glee!

Next day he kept his word, and though Miss Linda played a little while, somehow the spirit seemed to have gone out of her music. But when Arthur came out on all-fours from under the instrument's front, hot, red and tousled, his sister shook his little hand and thanked him and kissed him tenderly—and he, swelling with gratified pride and love, went out behind the smoke-house, where he swore a little for practice, and tried to kill the cat.

Next morning early, as I left our room, I glanced into Miss Linda's, and saw it had not been put in order yet. Being ever eager to do something in her service, I thought I might slip in and beat up her pillows and place them in the sun as I had seen the "grown-ups" do. So in I went and, snatching up the nearest pillow,

I gave a startled " Oh!" and stood staring, for beneath it lay the miniature of a man, whose questioning brown eyes looked up at me from a face young yet stern to the point of sombreness. My first impulse was to restore the pillow and run away, but next moment I noticed, lying close to the picture, all crumpled up into a little wad, Miss Linda's handkerchief. I leaned over and touched it, and it was still damp with tears. A great lump rose in my throat and, though I was but a "growing-girl," it was the heart of a woman that was giving those quick, hard blows in my breast and making me understand. I sprang across the room and softly closed the door. I said to myself: " Miss Linda loves him, and she is unhappy and grieves, and she does not wish them to know!"

I went to her bureau and took a fresh handkerchief from the drawer, then I took the miniature—it was on ivory, and, from its small, gold frame, I fancied it had been intended for an ornament—and slipped it into the velvet case I found near by; then I carefully rolled the case inside of the handkerchief and started down stairs, trying hard to look unconcerned as I entered the dining-room.

Breakfast had just been placed upon the table, and every one save Linda was moving toward it. A little, drooping figure still seated, she seemed very ill that morning, and the great, dark circles about her eyes looked like purple stains on her white face. I crossed directly to her, thus turning my back upon every one else, and leaning over her and thrusting my small package into her hand with a warning pressure of the fingers, I said: "I have brought a fresh handkerchief for you, Miss Linda—do you want it?"

The moment she touched the parcel she understood. Her eyes sent one startled glance toward her father—then she looked at me. The white weariness faded all away, and warmly, rosily I saw her love blossom sweetly in her face, while she answered: "Thank you, little sister—yes I want it," and slipped the handkerchief into the pocket of her gown, just as her father pushed me impatiently aside that he might assist her to her place at table.

He instantly noted the color in her face and sharply exclaimed: "What's this—what's this! is this a feverish manifestation, at this hour of the day?"

And Linda smiled and charged him with "cultivating his imagination, instead of his corn," and by the time she was in her place the color had faded, the waxen pallor was back upon her face, and the small incident had been safely passed.

Late that afternoon Linda was lying on, or perhaps I should say clinging to, the hard and slippery thing they called a sofa—Heaven save the mark! It was long and hard, and smoothly covered with shiny leather. It arched up in its middle over very powerful springs, and the springs and the slipperiness did the trick for every one. You could not snuggle on it to save your life, and if you attempted to be friendly with it and tried to rest your book or fan or smelling bottle beside you—hoop la!—with an intensity of malice known only to the inanimate enemy it would hitch up its back and fire everything off onto the floor well out of your reach—and if you showed any marked annoyance it would fire you after them. There was not a day that it did not shoot Miss Linda's pillow from under her head, and twice I saw it slide her bodily to the floor.

I had found just one thing that could hold on to this slippery fiend, and that was a blanket—but who on earth wanted to lie on a blanket in the summer time? So there Miss Linda lay on the glassy-surfaced "sofa," with a chair pushed close up to it to prevent her sliding off, and I on the floor slowly fanning her and hoping she might be asleep, she was so very quiet. But no, she was not sleeping, for presently, without opening her eyes or making the least movement, she whispered: "Little sister, you saved three of us much grief and pain by your caution and your thoughtfulness to-day, and now, dear, I will explain about the picture."

I turned hot and shame-faced, and rubbing my head upon her hands like an affectionate young puppy, I muttered confusedly, "that, if she pleased, I'd rather not!" But she smiled; not her family smile, but a sad, slow smile, and stroked my hair and went on gently: "It is right that you should know. He, the man of the miniature, was to have been my—" She stopped; she swallowed hard at something. She moistened her lips and started again: "He—at least, I was to have been his wife! I wore his ring—I—I—" Suddenly her eyes opened wide on mine, and she said with a sort of rush: " Child, child! Heaven will have to be a very glorious place to make me forget the happiness I knew with him! and I loved him so! oh, I loved him so!"

In a very transport of sympathy I broke in: " But he was good, I am sure he was! and he don't look as if he were dead?"

She smiled kindly at me, and fully understood my blundering, hurried words: " Yes, dear," she said, " you are right; he is not dead, and he is good! A little hard, perhaps—" Her eyes closed again. " Yes, perhaps, a little hard, but—well, men must be hard or they cannot succeed! We were very happy, dear! Papa—" Her brows drew together quickly for a moment; —" papa gave his consent. He—Roger—had a noble voice; we sang together at the church, we rode, we planned—we planned—" A pause, a long, long, shivering sigh, and then: " Papa changed his mind. I was not of age—even had I been, I had been bred up to such strict obedience—I—oh, I don't know!—but Roger, he could not bear dependence on another man's whims for two long years! He was one of the college professors; he needed quiet, regularity, positively settled plans, or the quality of his work might suffer! Papa broke his promise—he gave no reason. Roger said 'he was jealous of us.' I only know he broke his promise! Roger would not wait! Father commanded—he demanded! They were two angry men—I stood between them, dear—and I am crushed!"

"Oh," I cried, "he did not love you hard enough, dear Miss Linda! What was enduring two years of Mr. Hyler compared to enduring a whole life without *you?*" It was not exactly a polite way to speak of the reverend gentleman or of her lover, and she laid her finger on my lips, as she resumed: "Papa does not understand—time has passed—but, oh, child, child!—each day of my life—I lose my love—each day the pain of it—is fresh and new! Had papa known of the picture to-day—he might have understood—he might have—suffered remorse—and he is old and—and—'As we forgive those who trespass against us!'"

Her whisper died away on the last word; she lay quite still. I fanned her gently, slowly, and kissed her little, paper-dry hands now and then, and by-and-by the smile faded quite away, the sweet lips took a downward droop, the heavy waves of her brown hair made her face look piteously small and wasted, and, with hot tears dropping down into my lap, I took my first look at the real Linda. The little songster, with the song stopped in her throat! The loving little woman, with her heart crushed in her breast!—and as it was my first so it was my last look at that Linda, for it was the only time I ever saw her asleep, and when awake she was always on dress-parade, and wore her smile as an officer would his sword.

Shortly after this I began to worry, for though I was

still in ignorance, even I could see that as these hot days went panting by each one of them took with it some small portion of dear Miss Linda's strength. The dandelion in seed, lifting in air its phantom, downy globe, was scarcely whiter, lighter or more frail than she. Then I was worried about myself. The family were taking suddenly too deep an interest in me, my tastes and my desires. I was even asked what I would do under such and such circumstances, or how I would decide between this claim and that, and when I entered a room the " grown-ups " were almost sure, of late, to stop speaking, or they would clear their throats and speak of the weather with an elephantine lightness that could not deceive a goggle-eyed infant negotiating teeth with a rubber ring.

Once my very own mother, speaking excitedly, too, stopped short when I came in, and though I looked and looked at her with forty-horse questioning power in my eyes, she answered nothing, and my most penetrating and gimlet-like glance finally brought out a very brief, not to say sharp, suggestion that I sit down and stare at my spelling-book awhile—which, like most good advice, was neither kindly given nor willingly followed. So I was worrying, when one morning I stood listening to Miss Linda's unspeakably sad music. She was playing with fervor and more strength than usual, and suddenly she was seized with a paroxysm of coughing. Instead of going to her at once, I ran into the next room for some troches that were on a table, and before

I could return with them she had fallen and was lying motionless on the floor. My cry and the shouts of little Arthur gave the alarm. Mrs. Hyler entered first. She went very white, but she stooped and lifted Linda like a child, and I thought it strange that, as she carried her, she held a handkerchief to her face. Mr. Hyler appearing suddenly, exclaimed in excited tones: "Ice—ice! Salt—linen!" and, taking these exclamations as orders, I ran forward, intending to carry the message to my mother. At that moment Mrs. Hyler stretched out her hand to push the door more widely open, and on the breast of her light dress, just where Miss Linda's head was resting, a great, red stain was slowly, evilly spreading. I glanced from it to the handkerchief in her hand, and it was red! red!! red!!! With stiffening lips, I whispered: "Miss Linda—oh, Miss Linda!" and suddenly there came a mighty roaring in my ears—a cold air on my face, and as I sank into the windy darkness, afar off I heard a voice cry: "There she goes! Catch the child—ah! she saw it all."

Yes, in very truth I had seen all! And when, with a general sense of discomfort, I opened my eyes upon the sunlight again, I found myself attended by two of the seven sons, who cast water on me with lavish hand and pounded me with an affectionate brutality that left marks by which my fainting might be remembered for days after. I looked stupidly at them at first and wondered, and then I saw that great, red, growing stain beneath the wasted, white face, and I broke into such sobs as fairly frightened them. I was crouching on the top step of the porch, with my feet drawn up and my arms and head resting on my knees, and as I glanced downward I saw four bare, brown, boyish feet, and noted how restless they were. With my heart almost bursting with pain, some portion of my brain made a note of the fact that one of the four great toes before me had received a recent cut that must have been given by a hoe. Then the elder one thumped me kindly on the back and said: "Don't, Carrie, don't!"—and the other one said, in a husky voice: "Why, didn't yo' never know at all that sister Linda was agoin' to die?"

I gave an agonized cry at the words, and the elder boy exclaimed: "What did yer want to say that for? For two cents I'd give yer a good lickin'!"—while he, of the toe, said: "No, yer won't give me a lickin' for two cents, nor for one cent, neither!"

"Why won't I?"

"Why didn't Jack eat his supper, eh?"

And then they grabbed at each other over my head, but a grave voice said: "Boys, I never was so shamed by you before!"

It was Alfred, the eldest of the seven, and a "grown-up" himself. He paid no attention to their explanations—their recriminations; he simply stooped, and, lifting my shaking body in his arms, carried me into the house. As he was going up the narrow stairs a splash came on my cheek that was no tear of mine. A thrill went through me from head to foot—I lifted my swollen lids to look at him. His face wore that gray tint paleness brings to dark people, and in his always sad eyes I saw slow tears gathering. I buried my own face in his bosom, and laying my shaking, little hand across his eyes, I sobbed: "Don't, oh, please don't! She couldn't bear it if she knew!"

He took me to my mother's room and, placing me high against the pillows, deftly tied a wet handkerchief about my hot brows, and then he stood looking down at me for a moment before he said, with a quivering voice: "You know now, don't you, Carrie?"

I nodded my head and wrung my hands silently. "Yes," he went on, "she is going soon, dear—and—and—it's rough! Good God! Carrie! if you could have seen her three years ago—if you could have heard her sing! I think sometimes my father is a devil! There—there—I didn't mean to say that!—but see, dear, little girl!" He knelt down quickly by the bed and took my hands in his. He spoke rapidly—pressing my fingers tightly, to hold my attention: "They are going to ask you to do something—to-morrow, perhaps —this awful attack of Linda's will hurry things—I can't tell you *what* they will ask; I have not the time, but, Carrie, refuse! Don't be badgered—don't be coaxed—not even by darling Linda! One martyr is enough! Refuse, refuse! for, oh, we will be a hard lot when sister has left us!"

His body shook with sobs; for a moment he let his head rest on the edge of the bed. Then he rose and left the room to go to his own, where I heard him lock himself in. And that day ended my ignorance about Miss Linda's fate, and it also ended Miss Linda's music—she had played her last note.

That I had received a shock was evident to the whole family, and I heard the sick girl say to her father: "Wait, papa, dear, don't speak to Carrie yet—give her a little time."

But my grief was greater than my curiosity, and I never asked myself what he could have to speak to me about, or what he could possibly ask of me. I only thought of her—to fan her, hand her a drink, bring her a flower, carry a message, or, above all, during that afternoon hour, to crouch at her side and watch her "silent singing," as I called it. She never seemed to do it before her mother or any one but me. But while she was supposed to be taking a nap, and I fanned her quietly, she would lie, with closed eyes, and softly beat time with her shadowy hand, and her throat would swell and her lips move, but no sound came; and through much watching of her, with my heart in my eyes, I came to know what she sang. Often it was "Lead, Kindly Light," but more often, to my torture now, it was that expression of absolute submission, "Just as I Am, Without One Plea." And when her pale lips found the words, "O, Lamb of God, I Come," I would bite my lips and hold my breath, that I might not break into the wild sobs that would have sore distressed her.

I had not liked the Rev. Hyler at any time, but when I learned that, minister as he was, the sole religious observance for the family was a hasty, almost angry, snatch at a blessing on the food, while for visitors there were family prayers both night and morning, my dislike became marked. Linda saw it as she saw everything, and unable to defend him, she suffered and was ashamed, but kept silent until that hot afternoon, when she said: "Little sister, you are not fond of papa, but try, dear—to put out of your mind —that matter of the prayers, and only think how old and tired and tried he is—and" (I heard his step approaching, and his dry, little cough)—" and listen to him kindly—and try to do what he asks of you—try, dear, for all our sakes."

And then, to my bewilderment, the Rev. Hyler and his worn and helpless wife made solemn entry and seated themselves, and I, having risen respectfully, stood there and received the blood-curdling proposal that I should become the sister of the seven—the adopted daughter of the Rev. Hyler! Amazement kept me silent, and they went on to explain, with their eyes turned away from Linda's face, "how bad it would be for the boys to be without a sister's influence —and how they had been greatly gratified, though much surprised, to see that the younger boys had taken a strong liking to me," and, glancing at their two grim faces, I wondered what they would say or do if they knew that their boys' liking was founded upon a generous but downright falsehood, told by me to save the second youngest from a most unjust and cruel thrashing; after which I had gone at once to my mother, confessed the lie and accepted my punishment with a cheerful acquiescence that filled the seven with admiration and made them declare, with enthusiastic vulgarity, that I was "the biggest thing on ice!"

At last it dawned upon them that, for mere form's sake, they should ask an answer from me, and it came in a swift and emphatic "NO!" They were surprised and angry, but to all their half-sneering questions—as to why and wherefore—wide-eyed and amazed, I had but one word for answer: "Mother!" The Rev. Hyler answered: "My wife will be your mother!"— and I almost laughed; then with large conclusiveness I replied: "But my mother loves me, sir!"

Miss Linda caught my hand and said: "Think, Carrie—a home—brothers—father and mother to love you."

I looked at him a walking bitterness, I looked at her a withering disappointment and said: "No! no, dear Miss Linda, they love you, but they would not love me —and" I triumphantly added, "they will not tell you so!"

She turned questioningly to them, but the challenge was not accepted. Angrily her father bade me go, saying, "I might know what hunger was some day."

But I answered cheerfully: "Oh, I have been hungry sometimes, and so has mother, but we were together, so it was all right. You know when you're orphans and widows, you always come all right"—a speech that was as perfect in faith as it was imperfect in grammar.

The Rev. Hyler, with a vindictive gleam in his eye, "hoped I might be hungry again, that I might appreciate what I was rejecting"—and Miss Linda kissed me with a disappointed face, and whispered for me to go, now.

After that life became intolerable there, and soon there came a morning when, ready for an early start, I crept into Miss Linda's room and knelt down by her bed, and with hands tight-clasped we looked—and looked—and looked, and spoke not one word between us. Then there came a call for me, and I rose to go. As I bent over to kiss her, she lifted a thin, little, warning hand and tried to turn my face away, but with a smothered cry of indignation, I caught her hand and held it while I slipped my other arm beneath her incredibly frail shoulders, and lifting her, I kissed her shadowy hair, her brow, her cheeks and her pale, dry lips. Then with a long, long look into her dark, sapphire-blue eyes, I laid her down and went out, and saw her no more forever. As I closed the door gently behind me, I heard, for the last time, the husky whisper that had grown so dear to me, and all it said was, "Little sister!"

I stumbled down the stairs, and slipping my hand into my mother's, we faced the world once more, I having faith to believe that somewhere in its mighty length and breadth there was a home for us, and that together we should somehow find it.

For two years the gentle, little silent-singer had been lying in her lonely and neglected grave, when I paid my only visit to the Hyler family. Circumstances had brought me into the neighborhood, and I felt in duty bound to "pay my respects," as they called it. Poor Alfred's fear seemed to have been justified, for the neighbors declared that since Linda's death the boys had become a " hard lot," and seemed actually to be growing more boldly bad week by week.

The Rev. Hyler and his wife at first seemed to derive a sort of sour satisfaction from my visit to them. The boys received me with noisy greetings and many poundings on the shoulders, and young savages that they were, they expressed their hospitality by the making of gifts, such as horse-hair rings, matched jackstones, and several chunks of not-too-clean flag-root, both the smell and taste of which were particularly offensive to me.

Before tea was over all the kindness had gone out of Mrs. Hyler's face, and it began to wear the look I had known well in former days, of dull, sullen dissatisfaction. Suddenly, apropos of nothing, she said: "I suppose, Carrie, you have heard all about Linda?"

With some hesitation I answered: "Yes, I think

so. I heard that she—she went away in her sleep, and that you held her hand—but never knew when—"

"Oh yes," she broke in, angrily, "and they told you, too, that I had sat there asleep, or I would have known—I know their tales."

"Oh dear, Mrs. Hyler," I cried, "indeed no one ever implied such a cruel thing! They only said she passed so gently that no one could have known the actual moment."

She seemed somewhat mollified by this assurance, and went on more rapidly, and as she spoke she slowly turned her cup round and round in its saucer: "Linda had been so much better that last day that it seemed almost foolish when she expressed her wish to see each one of the boys alone for a few minutes. I told her so, but she only smiled and said, 'so much the better for the boys.' The memory of her last words to them should not be associated with suffering and pain, and so she had her way, and held each brother in her arms and whispered some last words—but smiling, smiling all the time."

I clasped my hands tight beneath the table, and my heart seemed to beat out those cruel words, "smiling, smiling all the time," and I whispered "Miss Linda, oh, dear Miss Linda!"

"Yes, and she had a little gift for each—and—well, later in the afternoon she was lying on the sofa, her eyes were closed, and beneath the cover her hand seemed to be moving all the time. Perhaps she was nervous, but she was saying, or repeating-to-herself-like, the words—"

I could not help it—from my lips sprang the line: "Just as I Am, Without One Plea!"

There followed a sort of general exclamation, and Mr. Hyler leaned forward, saying sharply: "How's this? Who gave you your information—not the boys, I'm sure?"

Hot and confused, I said: "Nobody told me, I had only guessed," (his disbelief was palpable) "because dear Miss Linda was so very fond of that hymn, and sang it nearly every day to herself."

And Mr. Hyler sneeringly assured me that, as Linda has lost her voice more than a year before her death, my statement had at least the element of surprise about it!" I sat mute—I could not explain to them about the silent singing.

Then Mrs. Hyler took up the hateful ball and sent it rolling toward me with the suggestion, "that as I was a good guesser, perhaps I had guessed all that she had been going to say?"

I steadied my voice and answered, respectfully, "that I had not guessed anything else," and with mock surprise she said: "Indeed?" and then went on: "After a silence Linda spoke of you, Carrie."

I looked up joyfully—my mortification all forgotten: "She said you were a remarkable girl"(even at that moment I was proud that she had not called me child, but "girl"). "I told her you were well enough, but in no way remarkable. She insisted, however, and then added, that if I ever saw you again I was to give you a remembrance. I thought the gift she chose very odd and unattractive, but she said" (how slowly she was speaking now) " she said you would understand it."

She paused so long that I looked up. Her eyes were like a ferret's, and Mr. Hyler, with his head in his hand, was watching me from between his fingers.

"Yes, ma'am," I whispered, faintly, vaguely. Then she spoke loudly, roughly: "She told me to give you a handkerchief, and say to you, the longer you lived the better you would understand her gratitude, for your *golden silence*."

I felt the blood fairly pushing through my veins— my downcast eyes noted that the very backs of my hands were turning red. Then Mrs. Hyler struck the table sharply and said: "Well, was she right—do you understand?"

I had no time to answer, for Mr. Hyler sprang up and, violently thrusting his chair against the wall, cried: " What folly to ask the question—of course she understands! Is not her knowledge burning red in her face?"

He stepped across the room and flung wide the door leading to his *study*, as he termed it—the boys called it " The Place of Horrors," because they were always thrashed there with peculiar malevolence and ingenuity, and generally unjustly—they seldom got punished when they deserved it. There he waved me in. But grave and stern, Alfred's voice came: "Father—father! Carrie is but a child—she is here alone, and she is a visitor!"

"Visitor or no visitor!" was the answer, "I will not permit this stranger, this mere nobody, to have knowledge of my daughter that is unknown to me!"

With wistful voice I meekly asked Mrs. Hyler: "Please ma'am, may I have the handkerchief?" and she sharply answered: "No—no! you shall have no handkerchief" (Alfred quickly left the room a moment) "until you have confessed every word that ever passed between you and Linda!"

Here Alfred came in again and, leaning over, placed in my hand the little gift, and kissing me, gently said: "There, Carrie, it was Linda's own!" Then as he passed his mother, he laid his hand on her shoulder and said: "Dear mother, it was not yours to withhold—we must all honor sister's wishes."

Mr. Hyler fairly shouted: "Take your seat and be silent, sir! As for you," (turning to me) "into that room! I will know what conduct my daughter was guilty of that she should be grateful for the shelter of your 'golden silence'!"

The four eldest boys sprang furiously to their feet, but the cry that rang the wildest in that room, that might have been the cry of a woman grown, came from my lips. I stood gasping a moment, and all I thought was: "Miss Linda, oh my Miss Linda—he insulted you—he—he, whom you always spared!" And then

A Silent Singer   29

I began to grow cold—bodily, mentally! My shamefacedness, my fear, all fell away from me. I must have gone very white, for No. 5, a rather timid, gentle boy, said lowly: "Oh, mother, will Carrie faint? She won't die too, will she?"

I lifted my eyes to the Rev. Hyler, and I felt a great contempt for him; while down deep in my heart there was growing a bitter anger that merged, at last, into a vindictive longing to see him suffer. I threw up my head and marched into "The Place of Horrors," and turning, waited for him to follow me. He paused and looked at me with the same gleam in his eyes that shone there the day he wished "I might know hunger again." Then, with petty triumph, he exclaimed: "When you leave this room I shall understand this thing!"

But he was only partially right, for when I left that room he understood several things. He banged the door shut, and then seated himself at his writing table, leaving me to stand at his opposite side, as a culprit stands before a judge. I looked at him and saw all the narrow, gray man's meanness, his eager curiosity that was like that of a scandal-monger's. Yet, I gave him one chance, for when he demanded: "Well, now, Miss?" I said: "Mr. Hyler, you *must* know, there is nothing wrong about dear Miss Linda's kind message to me—she simply—" "Stop, where you are!" he cried. "I'll have no prevarication! Where there is secrecy there is shame! No one ever conceals what is right!

I'll have the truth, now, and the meaning of this message!"

And I answered: "Yes, sir, you shall have the truth!" and I told him briefly of Miss Linda's silent singing, and of her undying sorrow for her lost lover. As I spoke, utter amazement grew upon his face—he stammered out: "Why—why—what are you saying? She never spoke of him! Why—nearly three years had passed—since—since—the—r—the break—and 'er— you don't know what you are talking about—she did not grieve!"

"Oh, yes, she did!" I tranquilly replied. "That was why she would never have a light in her room at night for fear the picture might be seen. She slept with it beneath her cheek, and washed it with her tears, and dried it with her kisses. Oh, yes, she grieved!"

His eyes began to look sunken and his face was working convulsively. Then I told him how I had found the picture and wrapped it in a handkerchief and had given it silently to her in his presence, and she had been grateful, not because she was ashamed of her love or her sorrow, but because she wished to spare him suffering. And with his clenched fist he struck the table, blow after blow, crying furiously: "You lie—you baggage—you lie!" Then suddenly turning his trembling hands palms upward, he pleaded: "Carrie—tell me that you lie!" But coldly I answered: "I do not lie at all, sir—and you know I do not— besides, here are dear Miss Linda's very own words:

"Every day of my life I lose my love—and every day the pain is fresh and new!"

His eyes roamed from side to side—little bubbles formed in the corners of his lips, his hand went up to his throat and tried to loosen his collar, and I could just hear the whispered words that left his lips: "Linda—Linda—Linda!" and then, I struck my last blow at him. (Oh, Miss Linda, to-day, I ask your pardon, but then I was hard and pitiless, as only the very young can be.) And I went coldl yon : "She said to me, she did not wish you to know of her sorrow, because, *perhaps* "—I leaned on the table and brought myself nearer to him—"*perhaps* you *might* feel remorse!"

He threw one hand above his head and gave a cry: "Perhaps? perhaps? only perhaps?" and suddenly fell forward on the table, with outspread arms, and I heard him call upon the God he had never truly served and ask the mercy he had denied his own child! And, as I left the room by a second door opening into the entry where hung my hat and cloak, the vindictive devil that possessed me made me say quite clearly: "As a father pitieth his own children!"

I was tying on my hat when I distinctly heard the boys quarreling as to whether or no there would be prayers held in my honor—some saying, "yes, because I was company," and the younger ones arguing that, as I was not a "grown-up," "there'd be no family prayers," then suddenly there was a howl, and I knew they were coming to blows.

I slipped from the house, without good-bye to any one, and as I passed the study window, I glanced in and saw the "gray head" bowed upon the table and two hands beating feebly, aimlessly, and suddenly I seemed to hear Miss Linda's husky whisper saying: "And only remember how old and tired and tried he is, dear!"

And I cried aloud: "Forgive me, forgive me, dear Miss Linda—I did it because I loved you so!" and looking across the years—I say now—I love you so, dear LITTLE SILENT SINGER.

An Old Hulk

An Old Hulk

Old Thomas Brockwell—sometimes called Bull Brockwell, he of the mighty thews and sinews—had been for some years a widower, and had he remained a widower I should have been the poorer by one good friend—a lowly one—oh, yes—but you know that true friendship is one of the few things the lowly can afford to give.

But the broad-shouldered, ruddy-faced old Briton had married an American wife in the person of the mother of my closest chum—and so I learned many things about the narrow, hard, honest old giant—things that sometimes filled my eyes with tears of laughter; sometimes with stinging drops of anguished pity. The only surprising thing about Brockwell's second marriage was that it had not taken place years before—for given a working-class Englishman of middle age—owning a house of his own—you have the worst material in the world for a widower. But, like most of his race, he was a bit contrary, and when all his housekeepers and his elderly unmarried friends pursued him openly— without even trying to hide the matrimonial *lasso* with a few flowers of sentiment or delicacy—he shook his obstinate, old head and plunged away.

Then Emily had arrived upon the scene, whom he described as "a fine figure of a woman" (she weighed something over two hundred), and if she was too inert to join in the general pursuit of him, she was also too inert to *avoid* pursuit herself—hence the marriage, and though, while praising her housekeeping, he openly expressed his doubts of her soul's salvation—the new, phlegmatic Mrs. Brockwell remained quite undisturbed. She was an experienced chewer of gum—she said she *had* to chew it to aid her digestion—but be that as it may, a certain mental clearness, a sort of spiritual calm, seemed to come to her from her steady, cow-like munching. On the occasion of her second marriage she had contentedly chewed until she took her place before the lean, old minister; then, having no bridesmaid to act for her, she stuck her gum on her breastpin, temporarily, while she promised to accept the big party at her side, and all his belongings, and to nurse him for the rest of his life without further remuneration—and with the nuptial benediction she had resumed her gum and had gone forth a slowly-chewing, contented bride—and on Sunday, he wishing, probably, to do all that was courteous and polite under the circumstances, took his new wife out to the cemetery and proceeded to introduce her —as it were—to the other members of the family.

A hideous chunk of stone stood in the middle of a plot, from which the graves rayed out like the spokes of a wheel—and old Thomas, with a cane, which so surely only appeared on Sundays that a bad little boy once said: "God made the Sabbath day and old Brockwell's cane!"—with this cane he immediately bored a little hole at the foot of one grave and remarked: "I buried my *first* wife there"—and Emily brought her jaws to with a snap, and bowed her head slightly, as though acknowledging an introduction. Then she chewed again, and old Thomas yanked out the cane with some effort, as though Mrs. Brockwell No. 1 was holding on to it. Then he bored another little hole at the foot of another grave with the cane and announced : " I buried my eldest son here "—another stoppage of the jaws and another bow—and so the old " borer " went on, till each member of the family had been presented to the new-comer in turn, and then he gave the final touch of brightness to this very original bridal outing by carefully measuring with the cane the space, to see if there was enough left for two more spokes to his family " wheel of death."

Mrs. Brockwell was wont to declare she would remember that day as long as she lived. Not because her sensibilities were wounded, but because she had not been constructed for rapid action, and she declared she would never have lived through the homeward walk but for the sustaining power of an extra piece of gum, which she luckily had in her pocket—for this was the golden age of the world when women still had pockets.

Old Thomas Brockwell narrowly—very narrowly— escaped being a religious monomaniac. Unquestionably sincere, his religion was yet a thing so warped and bitter as to fill most people with shrinking dread. He studied only the Old Testament, rarely reading the

New. In his ears the rolling thunders of Sinai drowned the gentle "Voice" preaching from the "Mount." He believed in a personal Devil—he believed in a material Hell.

I have never known anyone who got as much satisfaction out of the *whole* of his religion as he got out of Hell alone. He talked of it, thought of it, and, in regretful tones, told many of his friends that they were going *there*. All its accessories were dear to him. The "brimstone," the "burning lake" and that "undying worm," which seemed, in his imagination, something between a boaconstrictor and a Chinese dragon, while the "bottomless pit" not only gave him two words to roll sweetly under his tongue, but provided an ideal place to shake frightened little boys over at Sunday-school— for he labored faithfully Sunday after Sunday to frighten sinful youth into the church or the idiot asylum.

His God was a bitterly revengeful God! The Bible told him to fear Him and to obey His commandments. The base of his religion was "an eye for an eye—a tooth for a tooth!" He knew no "turning of the other cheek"—no "forgiveness of enemies," and many a time, in his efforts to show his disapproval of the loving, gentle, yet strong teaching of the New Testament, he blasphemed unconsciously. Few things made him so angry as to suggest "a Hell of remorse"—of "tortured conscience"—of "mental agony"—while a hint at "atonement"—a final winning of forgiveness—was a

An Old Hulk

rag so red as to set him madly charging through the harshest and most cruelly just punishments meted out in the Bible—and the worse one promised for the future—*Hell!* " And *their* future is *now!*" he would shout, with glaring eyes! " *Now*, do you understand? All these disobedient servants of the Lord are in fiery torments *now!* and *will* be forever! Ah! its a big place—a *mighty* big place!—far and far away bigger than Heaven! It has to be, there's so many more to go there!"

Night and morning he read a portion of the Bible, and prayed loud and long—and right there he came in conflict with his Emily. There was just one point they differed on—they did not quarrel, because Emily was too slow in speech. There's no comfort to be had out of a quarrel, unless it's quick—*very* quick; and if Emily had had her choice she would a good deal rather have died than try to be quick.

The point of difference between this otherwise peaceful pair was whether the chewing of gum was un-Christianlike and disrespectful when indulged in during family service. The first time he had caught her in the heinous act he had roared out: " Woman, have you no decency? Would you chaw the ten commandments up into a hunk of gum?"

Emily had mildly stated that she chewed " to keep herself awake," and after many struggles it had come to a compromise—she was only to chew while he read; *not* while he prayed.

Emily explained matters to me one day in this way: "You see, Mr. Brockwell, he gets riled up because I chew gum while he's reading gospel, but it's really his own fault; if he'd only read one chapter, like an ordinary Christian man! My father, now, was a deacon, and he never read mor'n one chapter at a time at family service; but Mr. Brockwell, when he gets a smiting people hip and thigh, and a raining down plagues and things; why, there's no stop to him; he goes right along over ever so many chapters—and I don't take to the stoning and the killing—and so I go off to sleep, unless I chew gum right hard. Why, never once since we've been married has Mr. Brockwell been satisfied with the 'Fall of Jericho' for one reading. On he goes, and tackles that city of 'Ai,' and I always feel sorry when that line comes about the 'men and *women* that were slaughtered bein' twelve thousand.' But, land sakes! it's all sweeter than honey to Mr. Brockwell—'specially the hanging of the king, and piling stones on his body for the beginning of an altar—nasty, bad-smelling idea I call it. *But* when Mr. Brockwell begins with them 'seven trumpets of rams' horns' I begin to chew hard, for I know there's a lot to be gone over before praying begins. If he'd read oftener about Hannah and little Samuel I'd keep awake. Ain't that a nice little Samuel on the mantel—his left foot's broken, but kneeling like that you'd never know it, unless you turn him around." That being the sort of tangent Mrs. Emily was apt to go off on during a conversation.

The old man might have lived without working at that time, but he held idleness as sinful, so he, without any feeling of shame, acted as night watchman in a large building down town. One winter there were many burglaries, and his employer grew a bit uneasy, knowing his was a tempting establishment and remembering that Thomas Brockwell was an elderly man. So he asked his watchman if he would not like to have some one to help him during the rest of the winter. And Brockwell was hot with anger and answered that he could take care of his employer's property, but he didn't want to protect some young nincompoop besides. "I am able to take care of any burglars that come my way. A man of the Lord can always lick a law-breaker," and looking at the really splendid old body of his watchman, the gentleman had laughingly declared he "believed old Brockwell would be up to two or three younger men!" and let him go his obstinate, lonely way, and like many another word spoken in jest, these words proved true.

One bitter night, after reading with great enjoyment of the prompt action of the bears in the taking off of those ribald little boys who had made unpleasant remarks about the scarcity of hair among the prophets (surprising how alike the boys of to-day are with the boys of the scriptural epoch), and had prayed till Emily had fallen asleep, with her face squelched in the seat of the chair she knelt by, and had awakened and acknowledged her fault. "For," as she said to me, " after he had fallen over my legs without waking me, he might have thought I was lying if I had said I was just thinking."

And I had quite agreed with her and complimented her on her truthful nature—and he had taken his tin pail of coffee in his mittened hand and his package of sandwiches in his pocket and gone forth to his night's watch. He had been a sailor in his early manhood, and, in addition to the tattooed anchor and star on the backs of his hands, he still retained a few words from his sailor's vocabulary which he used now and then with bewildering effect upon the landsmen. Mrs. Brockwell found that habit particularly trying. She was one of those women who always get drabbled when they walk. Long street dresses were worn in her day, and had she possessed six hands instead of two, she would have failed still to keep her dress out of the wet or the mud. On Sundays when she was crowded into her best gown and was clutching her skirt in the most useless places, trying to pick her way across a muddy street, old Thomas was wont to exclaim from the rear: "Take a reef in the la'board side of your petticoat, Emily!" and Emily would hoist high the right side instead, and the left would go trailing through the mud, while the old man pounded the walk with his Sunday cane, crying: "La'board—la'board—la'board, not sta'board. Now just look at your sails! Oh, woman, the ignorance of you at forty-six, not to know your la'board from your sta'board side!" And meek

Emily never suggested that left and right were the generally accepted terms for use on shore.

And as old Thomas walked through the biting cold, he congratulated himself on the honesty his wife had shown in admitting she had fallen asleep during prayers, and said to himself that it was the end of *her* day's work and he supposed she was tired—and—"great guns, how cold it was!" And so he maundered on and reached his store and entered and made his rounds, and finally at about two o'clock he took his coffee from the heater and began to drink it, when he paused—to listen. Then he put the coffee gently down and stole softly to the office—and saw two men at the safe, and with a cry, "Avast there!" he was upon them, striving to grasp them both! The smaller one was like an eel and had slipped from his clutch, but the larger one he held on to, and after a short struggle, he got his head "in chancery." He had just put in a couple of good blows—when he heard an ominous click behind him—at the same instant the man he was pounding fiercely growled: "No, no, don't use the 'barker'—you fool, you'll 'jug' us all yet! Choke the devil off, so I can do something—choke him, I say!"

With beautiful obedience and the spring of a wild-cat, No. 2 was on Brockwell's back, and doing his best to carry out orders. But it was that neck—that had given rise to the name *Bull* Brockwell; and the small ruffian tried in vain to get his clever thief's fingers in a choking grasp about the massive throat; but his weight was disturbing and distressing, and old Brockwell loosed No. 1 for a moment, while he reached up and tore the incubus from his shoulders. In the effort he wheeled half round and found himself facing a third man in the doorway. He had just time to note that the man had a bull's-eye lantern in one hand, some weapon in the other, and wore a half-mask on his face —when he received a crushing blow upon the head. He felt the hot blood leap forth in swift response to that savage gash. He staggered a bit, too, but did not fall, to the amazement of the brawny scoundrel, who exclaimed: "Well, I'll be damned!" Those words were like a veritable "slogan" to old Brockwell. "Aye, aye," he cried, "right you are, my hearty! Damned you will be, sure, and the burning lake of brimstone you'll get for this night's work!" and then they were upon him. He threw No. 3 out of the doorway and took that place himself, thus keeping all of them before him, and like an old bear "baited" by a pack of snapping, snarling dogs, he was slowly driven back until he found himself in the room again where stood his coffee. While he placed many blows where they would do the most good, still a great many more had fallen short. He felt his wind was going, and the streaming blood from his head impaired his sight, and just at that moment of threatened weakness the little thief struck him in the face, not with his fist but with his open hand—slapped him, in fact. With a roar of rage, old Brockwell caught up the pail and dashed the hot coffee full into his assailant's face, then shouting, "You little whelp, you cur, you worm!" with a mighty blow he drove the tin pail hard and tight on to the thief's head, half cutting off his ears with its rim, and as the other men made at him, by a happy fluke, he caught each man by the back of the neck and with every ounce of power to be had from his great arms and shoulders, he drove their two heads together in a smashing blow, and dropped their bodies as a well-bred terrier drops the rats he has shaken the life from. Then he turned for the little foe, just in time to catch upon his arm the blow that had been meant for his heart, and, by the hot smarting of his skin, he knew he had been cut by the little ruffian, whom he hammered into submission easily. Then Bull Brockwell sounded his whistle at the door for the police, and when they came he laid his hand on one of the officers' shoulder and faintly asked: "Why—don't—you—hold still—officer? You keep—going up—and down—," and then old Thomas went down, and for a time knew neither prayer, nor burglar, nor even burning brimstone, but only darkness.

When his senses came back to him he gave an exhibition of what might be called pig-headed honesty. There was a drug store and a doctor's office about two blocks away, and the policeman, on seeing the sorry condition of the old man, urged him to go and have his hurts cared for. *They* would see that all was safe during his absence, but he refused point blank, saying: "If a man was a watchman, he watched! If he was a night watchman he watched till the night was gone, or deserved the 'cat.' His employer paid him to stay in that building till daylight, and he'd stay, and be tended to afterwards."

Half angrily the policeman exclaimed: "You obstinate, old bull! Do you want to bleed to death, then?" And the "bull," with some embarrassment, had acknowledged that he did not really desire death, but with a sigh of satisfaction, he suddenly announced: "The Lord will settle all that. All I've got to do—is my duty—and though I don't feel just what you might call—hearty—I—I—guess—I'll hold out—till time's up and—" and his gray white lips trembled into silence.

The policeman, finding him immovable in his determination, sent for help, and soon the battered "old Brockwell" was being washed and strapped and bandaged and stitched, and had a few feet of plaster over some strained muscles, and was generally "made over." And then the stunned burglars had recovered their scattered senses and received a smiling and joyous welcome from the policemen, such as is only offered when the lost is found—and indeed one of these gentlemen had been lost—from the penitentiary—for several months. When the party of three were rounded up, ready for an early morning stroll to the station house, No. 1 had turned to Brockwell and growled:

"See here, you old slugger, next time I come up against you just hit me over the head with a loaded cane, or the butt-end of a revolver or something *soft* like that, will you? I don't want to be 'put out' no more with another 'mug's' head, now I tell you fair!"

"A—a—ah!" cried the little fellow, "he's a fightin' freak, he is! He ought to be a doin' time for jamming a tin pail over a man's head and half cutting off his ears!"

And so they went forth, cursing the night they had tackled "old Bull Brockwell!"

And then he had returned home, "sans buttons et sans reproche," and finding a barrel of flour standing at the side door, had picked it up and carried it into the house, apparently to convince himself that he was not much hurt. Then, beginning to feel stiff and lame, he put himself into Emily's hands, and she promptly put him into his bed, and scrambled through the "Fall of Jericho," stuck her gum upon the bed-post while she did it, then she had looked at his head and said, "she'd no idea a man could sew so neatly!" and then old Brockwell got hot and feverish, and his eye and cheek had blackened, and the doctor said he must be kept quiet a few days, at which dictum Emily had groaned aloud: "Kept quiet? Him? Good Lord!"

And, truly, had she been alone with him those days, her work would have been cut out for her. The ideal "bull in a china shop" would have proved an inoffensive and lymphatic creature compared to this pawing, plunging, irritable old Bull Brockwell! Bad enough at any time, when his eyes had swelled so he could no longer by the aid of his Bible put women and children to "the edge of the sword," nor erect altars, nor even calculate the dollars' worth of a " wedge of gold of fifty shekels weight," he proceeded to fret himself into a fever, and I was moved partly by pity and partly, I am sorry to say, by a spirit of mischief, to seat myself by his side, and with the air of one who carefully selects a soothing and pleasant topic for sick-room conversation, I brought forward the subject of eternal punishment, and for my reward had his fixed attention in a moment.

For a time he expatiated on the strong points of that place of torment, seeing no inconsistency in *paving* with broken promises a *bottomless* pit, and as he began to run down, assuming the air of one eager for information, I asked his opinion of that place of eternal coldness—that frozen lake.

"Coldness—coldness?" he repeated, "Why, I don't seem to remember!" and then another thought came to him and he broke out: "Fine! Splendid! I never felt such pain in my life as when I went near a fire with my frosted hands. Cold *and* fire! That's good! Ah, it would have been better to have respected them commandments—only ten of 'em too!"

Egged on by his evident satisfaction, I went on introducing to him "circle" after "circle" of the great Italian's Vision of Hell, and if Mr. Thomas Brockwell ever knew a genuinely happy afternoon, *that* was the one. And when I got a soft pencil and made black lines about the inside of his shaving-mug to illustrate the idea of the " circle," he eagerly peered in with his nearly-closed, discolored eyes and triumphantly cried: " And the old, burning-brimstone lake right at the bottom—eh ?"

All the punishments had met with his hearty approval save one. That great, black, " windy horror," through which unfortunate lovers beat their blind way—seeking, eternally seeking their sinful mates—met with instant condemnation. " If they had sinned—they had broken a very important law—a law, mind you, that Moses had received direct from Heaven. Just flying round in the dark was no punishment for such a sin! They got worse than that when they were alive!" For, you see, the old man was very material, and he failed to imagine the anguish of that " eternal, loving, despairing search!"

All went well. Old Brockwell not only kept to his bed, but enjoyed himself until night and time for family service arrived, and then the " snag" appeared in my way that I should have seen from the first. Suddenly suspicious, he placed his hand on the book and asked: " Just in what part of ' this ' did you find all that new ' Hell ' you've been telling me about, lass ?"

I sat stupidly silent. I had a vision of myself being driven away as unworthy to enter in with true believers, having jested upon the great subject. I tried to force my lips to speak, to tell him I would bring the book I had read it all in—but, truth to tell, I was too frightened to speak, and his brow blackening with anger, Mattie, his step-daughter, calmly asked: "Mother where was it in the old-world they found those 'sacred' manuscripts the other day?" (Poor Emily wasn't at all sure there was an old-world.) Mr. Brockwell, you'll know—Egypt wasn't it? Those wise men are working over them, you know, to translate them; they say they are parts of the old—"

"Egypt," declared the battered Brockwell. "Egypt, and very interesting they are too!"

"But," I meekly started, "but"—then Mattie cleared her throat loudly, and bending over me, muttered: "Don't be a fool—leave well-enough alone!" and I followed her advice and was silent. A month later, I told them "good-bye," my profession taking me far from them, and I could not help admiring the upright, powerful figure of the old man, as he stood at his gate—so perfectly proportioned that it was hard to believe that he was inches over six feet in height. As I reached the walk I looked back. Emily, large and buxom, stood in the door, a soft, red shawl about her ample shoulders —her jaws working with a slow precision that told me plainly she was "breaking in" a new piece of gum. Bull Brockwell waved his hat to me, and, against the westering sun, he loomed up black and big! And I said to myself: "In faith as in body—a giant!"

Three years had passed before I saw him again, three vivid, crowded years for me! Success had perched upon the lonely, little banner I had carried into that strange compaign where each one fights according to his own individual plan, and I was back in the old city, and because of that success was in great haste to seek my lowly, old friends out—for self respect, even a suspicious pride, renders it very hard for the lowly to make the first advance toward one who has risen ever so slightly. I had heard nothing of them during my absence, and standing at the door waiting a good, long wait—for Emily, like most large bodies, moved slowly—I said to myself: "I shall not see the dear, old 'Bull' for a couple of hours yet, as he will surely be sleeping now, but by six o'clock—" and then the door opened, and Mrs. Emily was before me, quite unchanged—and had taken me into a big comfortable embrace—and kissed me warmly and loudly, and expressed her gratification so noisily that I wondered she was not afraid of waking her husband—and then she led the way to the sitting-room, without one word of warning or explanation —which was so like Emily—and crying out, "My, Mr. Brockwell, but here *is* some one you'll be glad to see," she moved aside and left me in the doorway, where I stood quite still, the smile of welcome drying stiffly on my lips, while with pained astonishment I stared at— Mr. Brockwell (?)—oh, yes; that thick thatch of hair was neither whiter nor thinner than before. There was the splendid, old torso with all its depth of chest and breadth of shoulder. But why was he in that dread wheel-chair? Why were his great limbs covered with a quilt?

and, worst of all, why that strange expression in his face? Meeting that piteous, appealing glance, I felt the tears begin to fall, for I realized that in spite of the presence here of Mr. Brockwell—old Bull Brockwell was no more! The painful silence was broken by the trembling voice of Emily: "Father, I clean forgot to tell her—anything—and—and, I declare, she does take it right hard—don't she, now?" and she slipped out of the room, wiping her own eyes furtively as she went!

As I crossed the room toward him, his chin sank upon his breast, and shaking his old head slowly, he sadly murmured: "From him that *hath not*, shall be taken away even that which he *hath!*"

I took his great hand between both of mine, and my lips were just forming the words: "Surely this is but temporary?" when he raised his eyes, and, looking into them, I saw that hope was dead and buried there. I sank upon my knees beside him and said: "Tell me about it, Mr. Brockwell." He glanced towards his wife's room, but I persisted gently: "No—I want you to tell me," for my true sympathy had bridged the years between us, and we were like old friends.

In low tones he told his simple, commonplace story. It was the construction he put upon the usual that made it seem unusual, and brief and simple as his story was, it was intensely characteristic. He had started earlier than usual to his night's work, and was swinging his coffee-pail to the measure of the old hymn, "On Jordan's Stormy Banks I Stand," when, turning into a cross-street, he found himself in a crowd of running men and women, and in a few moments was in the midst of all the turmoil and commotion attending a fire, and he soon saw there was cause for the cries of the women and the curses of the men. There had been a nasty accident, and it had come to the first engine approaching the fire. It had been a case of strange driver and a too-short turn, and there, in a terrible heap, lay one horse flat, the other on its knees, and behind them a partly overturned engine. Worst of all, not only were its own services lost, but it was keeping other engines from entering the street, save by a long detour. Now, if ever there was a demand for lifting-power that demand was made right there, and old Brockwell sat down his coffee-pail and began to remove his heavy coat (it was early November then), when he learned quite suddenly that the burning house was a haunt of evil doers, was in fact a place that honest folk turned their faces from as they passed, and for the moment he hesitated, then flinging his coat fiercely off, he shouted: "Help! men, help! That fire *must* be quenched, to give those people one last chance to save themselves from eternal fire," and the "old Bull" was with the firemen, working with a will and showing such splendid lifting-power that the crowd cheered the "gray old Hercules" lustily, and among other happenings some "company's hose" had burst, and many were wetted thoroughly, among them old Brockwell. A church clock had boomed out the hour, and it was time for him to go on to his work, and then he felt how wet he was. He might have gone home and changed his clothing and only have been a little late in getting to the store. There was no one to make comment or to report his action, but he would be late, and he was proud, (the old man's lips had twisted painfully in uttering that word), proud of his punctuality, and—well—he had gone on to the store, wet as he was, and the night had been long, and now and then, strange, deep, burning pains, that seemed a mile long, had run from hip to heel, but he had watched the night out—and —and he would never watch again—that was all. He had, in fact, " scuttled his own ship," but in ignorance, lass! In ignorance, not in villainy. Yes, it was rheumatism first. He hadn't minded that so very much, because he had the awful pain to fight, but *this* (again that piteous twist of the lips), *this* partial paralysis—well there was nothing even to fight now.

Had I not seen hope dead in his eye? His head sank low on his breast. I touched my lips to his hand, and whispered, "How you have suffered!" His eyes closed wearily, and he answered lowly: "I have eaten ashes like bread, and mingled my drink with weeping," then, almost with a sob, he said: "Aye, aye—in very truth my sin hath found me out!"

I started almost angrily, exclaiming: "Your sin? What sin? You have loved—at least you have feared God all your life long! His word has ever been upon your lips. You have striven to obey His laws—what sin has found you out?" He raised his head, crying: "And to think I was so blind—so self-satisfied! To think how I tried to keep the boys from going to perdition by way of Sunday ball, and the girls by way of their vanity in their bits of ribbons! The blind 'leading the blind,' in good truth! Even when I was stricken I did not understand, until a neighbor made my sin plain to me."

"Ah," I said, "and had that neighbor removed the beam from his own eye, that he could see so very plainly the mote in yours?"

"I do not know," he answered, "but he said that pride went before a fall. And when I looked a bit surprised he added, 'you have been eaten up with vanity and puffed up with pride all your life, because of your great strength,' and oh, lass! lass! I was sore ashamed! Ah, well, I have no strength to sin with now—I am just naught but a useless, old hulk, or what is worse, 'a derelict!'"

"No," I said, "a 'derelict' is a menace and a floating danger to many men—you are no derelict!"

But he, shaking his clenched hand above his head in impotent sorrow, went on: "Worse! I'm worse than a danger to men! Men are strong and can save themselves, but here I hang like a mill-stone about the neck of that poor woman there—my wife, and she'll have to bear the dragging and the weight for years and years. For, mind you, I'm not like to die. The doctors say these things inside of me that they call 'organs' are all sound and strong, and that a man lives *by them*, not his legs, and so I'm to sit here rusting away, and watching her grow sick at the sight of me!"

Two slow, difficult tears stood chill and unshed in his eyes, and I felt, with a pang, how great must be the storm of sorrow that could cast its spray into those stern, old eyes.

"I don't suppose," he went on, "that she realizes it yet; she's good as gold. She takes care of me, helpless as I am, always just as smiling and pleasant, and sets right by me, and don't even go to church—just talks a little over the fence with the neighbors, so she can come and tell me what's going on. Why, she even offered to give up gum, and she a needing it for her digestion so, 'cause she thought it might make me restless-like (and there is a kind of gum, you know, that squeaks a good deal when it's new); but I ain't so selfish as all that. But, oh, if I could just die decently, as a man should when he's no more use, and not be a burden and a drag! For, you see, Emily's a mighty fine figure of a woman, and she might easily find a new home, with some good, sound man for a husband—who would protect her, and not sit, as I do, waiting for the day to come when his wife will look at him with loathing."

"Mr. Brockwell," I cried, "do you know that you are cruel to yourself and unjust to your wife?" He looked hard at me, but made no answer. "Your wife was always proud of you!" His face quivered—I had struck a wrong note—I hurried on: "proud of your character and standing, and of the pretty, little home you had so hardly earned, and now, oh, believe me, dear old friend, I know her heart better than you do yet—now she is proud to be the world for you, to be your feet, your nurse, your companion, your friend as well as wife."

He sadly shook his head: "She is a slave," he said. "Yes, if you will, she is a slave to her love for you, therefore she is a happy slave. You have said, yourself, that she smiles on you constantly. She never looked better in her life, and why does she call you 'father' now?"

His face brightened a little. "Yes," he answered, "she has called me 'father' ever since the—the—(how he shrank from the word) since the paralysis came upon me—yes, ever since."

"And," I went on, "can't you see what that means? She used to call you Mr. Brockwell—but when your cruel affliction came upon you she felt the absolute need of some term of endearment, because she loved you. Still, with the perversity of unhappiness, he exclaimed: "But Emily didn't say that. She never told me that she—she—"

"Oh, indeed," I broke in, "and have you given her a chance to tell you? Have you ever asked her if she loved you still?" And the old man, with a mind full of clean and wholesome memories, blushed at the question with a swift swirl of color in his cheeks that a girl of eighteen might have envied. "Have you?" I persisted. "Come, now, let us have a little fair play. You know she can't speak first. You know that, like every other modest, self-respecting woman, she must be dumb about her feelings—her emotions, until the man breaks the silence. You know she has been trained to silence from her earliest girlhood. Yet, knowing all that, you gnaw your heart in bitterness, because she does not dare lay her arms about your neck and assure you of her faithful love."

His eyes glowed, his great hands opened and shut nervously. He stammered and stumbled over his few words: "You think I haven't steered a straight course with Emily, eh? You actually believe, if I take a new tack, eh?—if I tell her how I—how,—well, how things are with me—that she'll come around to the helm—I mean—" and then suddenly his face fell and, shaking his fist in impotent rage at his helpless limbs, he cried: "Oh, she can't, she can't! Look at the miserable 'old hulk,' just rottin' slowly away between the tides of Time and Eternity, and talk of a woman lovin' it—a-a-h!"

I saw Emily's troubled face at the door and swiftly waved her away. Then I said, as brightly as I could: "Well, all 'hulks' are not despised! I saw a real one a few weeks ago!" He looked up quickly. "Where?" he asked.

"By the sea," I answered. "What kind of a hulk

was it—some unfinished failure of a 'tub,' I suppose?"

"No, a wreck! A great, gaunt-ribbed thing; stately even in its ruin. The waves—" He caught my dress as I rose to my feet. "Tell me about the 'hulk,' lass, tell me!" He pleaded just as a child pleads for a story.

"Very well," I said, "I'll tell you, but you must let me go to the spare room to lay off my hat. I'm going to stay all night, if your wife will let me!" I laughed at his request "for me to hurry," and said: "Mr. Brockwell, before I go, I want to say just one more word about your wife. *You* may doubt, but I am certain, *certain*, that should you have your cruel wish and die to-morrow, and should Emily be spared for many, many years to come, at the very end she will lie at your side, and will carry your name to her grave; and as I passed Emily I whispered eagerly: "Don't be angry with me; I'll explain later, but, for God's sake, go straight to your husband and kiss him!" The tears rushed into her eyes—she nodded her head and passed into the room where he sat.

I loitered long over the removal of my hat and wrap; I even waited to bathe my reddened eyes, and then, as I slowly descended the tiny staircase, Emily's voice, mildly indignant, came up to me, crying, "Oh, father, how could you, how could you?" and from the deep, bass rumble that followed there escaped these words: "A mighty fine figure of a woman, Emily!"

Then I sneezed loudly and entered the room to find them discussing the rival merits of " beaten " and " raised " biscuit, one of which we were to have for " tea." Mrs. Brockwell, being of a slow and peaceful nature, naturally preferred " raised " biscuit, but Mr. Brockwell, being more aggressive, took a great interest in the " beating " process. Once he asked, indeed, if *he* might not beat the dough, and Emily delightedly assented, putting a big, white apron about him and bringing everything close to his chair. But the poor, old giant's second blow had split the bread-board, and that had been the end of biscuit-beating for him. While Emily was pounding vigorously, if somewhat slowly, at her dough, I told my old friend of that other hulk, bleached white as chalk by the blazing sun, lying high upon the beach, listing over so that it made a sort of shelter for people to sit under, with the fine, pale sand slowly filling it—slowly piling up about it ; how, when I saw it, the ocean which had cast it there was stretched out waveless beneath the sun, with only a slow, deep, regular heave, that was like the breathing of some mighty monster at rest. I told him of that awful night when the signals of distress were sent up into the pitiless sky, and were seen and heard by helpless, distracted men and women on shore ; and how, in the gray morning, they were astounded to see the big ship high upon the beach, and dumbfounded when they saw she was a coffin, for there was the body of a woman there. Slight and young and small of foot and hand, and a Catholic, since a "scapula" was about her neck—and that was all. How the young stranger had been buried on the high land overlooking the sea and the wreck, and how, down below and up above, both were waiting, one for utter destruction, the other, for a glorious resurrection; and meantime the old hulk had become not only a landmark, but a thing beloved. Oh, yes; he need not shake his head, for that old hulk was the loyal friend of all true lovers. The great, gray, maimed thing sheltered many a shrinking pair from prying eyes. Brown, young rustics, who were fairly stricken dumb in the "sittin'-rooms" of their sweethearts, here, in the velvety, black shadow of the friendly, old hulk, found their tongues, and told swiftly and well the one old story that is ever new; while, as to summer nights—why, the old hulk was the trysting-place of lovers from half the countryside. It was so public, and yet so sheltered—so protecting. And it was so wise, the gray, old, sand-filled thing—it knew so much of Love, and Love's dear brother, Death!—so much—good God, so much! and yet was silent—ever silent!

Half the young married women of the little town had received their engagement rings within the sheltering arms of the old hulk, and some of them had carried their little children there, later on, that they might take their first, uncertain steps upon the soft, pale sands that were drifting ever higher about the bleaching wreck, just as one might take the first spring blossoms to some spot that was sacred to us.

That noble ship that on even keel, with mighty spread of snowy canvas, had sat the water a living thing of strength and beauty, had had a commercial value only, but wrecked, it had become a precious thing to them all, garlanded with the tenderest sentiments of both men and women, draped with the radiant hopes of youth, and each day gilded anew with ever-living love. As it sank deeper in the sand, so it sank deeper in their memories—their beloved "old hulk"!

The old man had listened so closely to my story that I was somewhat puzzled when he remarked on my last word: "If I was sure and certain that Emily was telling the truth about that patchwork, I don't know but what I might get to be more that sort of hulk myself, lass! If I could just be of a little use—ever so little, but real! —I could get along, but I don't want to be fooled, like a child, into doing *useless* things. The Lord says: 'A man should rejoice in his work!' but a man can't rejoice if it's only make-believe work!"

I began dimly to comprehend, and, proceeding cautiously, I remarked "that it would not be easy to deceive him, and I did not believe anyone would try!" He looked doubtful and, lowering his voice so that his wife might not hear him, asked: "You know what a master hand Emily is at piecing patch-work, don't you?"

I did know! I recalled the really handsome quilts she had shown me. It was the only way she had to gratify her natural love of color, and the workmanship was exquisite. The quilting in "fan" and "shell" and " diamond " forms equalling the piecing. Indeed, patch-work was a fine art in Mrs. Brockwell's hands. " Yes, I knew ! "

Then his keen, old, blue eyes took fast hold upon mine and, in an aggressive tone, he made this astonishing statement : " Well, Emily can't cut out any of her patch-work herself. She can't cut any two pieces exactly alike, to save her life ! " Oh, Emily, Emily ! poor, bungling, loving Sapphira ! I understood and thought fast while those piercing, old eyes held me ! I tried to laugh naturally, as I exclaimed : " Well, there's a pair of us, then ! I have lovely pieces—enough for two quilts, but I can't cut pieces alike, and am ashamed to ask any one to do it for me ; so there they lie ! "

" Oh, you ! " he impatiently answered, " but Emily, now ! " I thought of those quilts upstairs, while he went on : " See this thing, now ! " He pointed to the small quilt over his knees. I required no invitation, goodness knows ! for the ugly, ill-made thing had forced my attention long ago. No two pieces matched in length ; they were puckered and stretched (the old man called them " we-wahed ").

" That's *her* cutting," he announced ! I was about to explain, when I saw Emily behind him in the kitchen door frantically signing me to keep quiet. " Oh, dear ! " I moaned to myself, " what about those quilts upstairs ? "

" Yes ;" he went on, " that's a woman's cuttin' out ! Yes (argumentatively), I saw her do it ! And think of those quilts upstairs! (Ah, I thought!) Why, Emily says she would have had enough for herself and for her daughters' marrying, if she could have got her first husband to cut her pieces for her! (O, Emily!) but she had to beg and beg, and he wouldn't cut a single piece for a whole year sometimes. She says he was ashamed to do it, she reckons! Well!" he hotly ejaculated, " I'm not ashamed to do *anything* for *my* wife, unless "—he cooled suddenly again— " unless she's only making believe so as to give me employment!"

"Well," I said, "if you choose to doubt your wife, after looking at that awful quilt, you may. But you can't well suspect *me*, and if you will cut pieces for one quilt for me I'll give you silk enough for a quilt for yourself. Will you do it?"

The last suspicion faded! He threw back his head and laughed: " Will I? You'll see! Say, lass, just step over to the sta'board side of that sewing machine and hand me up that cuttin' board, and I'll show you what's the matter with the 'cuttin' out' of all you women. You see,"—he spoke with an air of growing authority as he unrolled some bits of calico—" you will just have your pattern cut out of a bit of cotton or delaine, and then you smack that down onto, perhaps, *several pieces* of goods together, never mind whether bias or straight, just to save time. Great guns! save time! Look at *that* thing over my knees! Well, *I* take the 'sun observation,' and I get my pattern all right, and *then* I cuts her out in good, stiff pasteboard, ma'am, and if it's a hard pattern, like ' bride in the mist ' or ' the risin' sun,' I have the thing cut out of a thin sheet of tin. A—a—ho! I don't make no mistakes, even with ' brides in the mist,' when I've a good, tin pattern to work by!"

As so often happens, enthusiasm was too much for his grammar. He talked and planned all through tea and right along to bed time, and I carried the big Bible to him and placed it open upon his lap. His hand instinctively began to turn the leaves in the front of the volume, but I rested my hand on the place I had selected, and, laughing, I said: "You have chosen for three whole years, *I'm company* to-night, and you must let me choose!"

He laughed a little and yielded, but when he saw my choice was from the New Testament, he frowned heavily, then cleared his brow as with an effort and read. He was not so familiar with the script as usual, and he read slowly and carefully, and when he came to that gentle, generous invitation and that all-comprehending promise, "Come to me *all ye—all ye—*who are weary and heavy laden—and I will give you rest!" he stopped! To this day I believe I felt the old man's thought, which was of the astounding comprehension by Jesus of his one craving wish—not for great joy—not for the inheritance of the earth—no, not for anything but that which was promised: "*Rest.*"

"Come unto me all ye who are weary and heavy laden, and I will give you rest!" Slowly, with trembling lips, he repeated the words a second time. Then he leant forward, tore a bit from the evening paper, and placing it as a marker, he closed the book. Emily and I knelt, and for once I felt no sense of the ridiculous in hearing a poor, finite creature explaining matters to the Infinite Being who knows all things. Very humbly the old believer explained to the God he had made so fearsome to himself why he lifted his voice in prayer in this unseemly attitude, instead of on his knees in humble, *loving* humility!

I gasped—I felt Emily's hand slip over and grasp mine—which proved lucky later on. Never before had that word been heard in that way, in this house of faith. But, oh, when the old man asked forgiveness for having wickedly doubted for a time the perfect truthfulness of one very near to him—his truest friend—Emily gave a plunge and tried to pull away from me. "I can't," she gasped. "I can't bear it! I must confess my lie!"

"Oh!" I moaned under cover of his bass rumble, "keep still! He's so happy now! Confess to heaven!" She tried again to pull her hand away. I clung tight, and putting my lips close to her ear, whispered: "*He* will forgive you because of your love! You know," I muttered wildly, "much shall be forgiven because she loved much! That's not it, but you know what I mean!"

The bass rumble stopped suddenly—so did I—but thank heaven, Emily's spurt of remorseful courage was over—her loving falsehood unconfessed! The rumble was resumed, and all was well!

Next day, as I came in hatted and cloaked to say "good-bye," old Brockwell—bright and ruddy—had his cutting board on his knees, bits of calico all over him. A foot-rule, a blue pencil, and several envelopes before him, and the air of "this is my busy day" of a railroad magnate at least. His "log-cabin" pattern had been found in a "rocky-mountain" envelope, and in fact things were all at loggerheads—but by and by they would be ship-shape. I was just to wait till I saw some of his *own* designs! Emily was going to go right *at* one—of "anchors"—blue anchors on a white ground, and did I suppose any of my pieces would be long enough—he couldn't well have those anchors less than six or seven inches long, and then a bit of the old Adam came out in him, when he lowered his voice to tell me: "*He* was not ashamed to cut patch-work, and he was not afraid—that in a year from now there would be quilts *down stairs* that could outsail anything up stairs that had been cut out only after beggin' and coaxin'!"

I looked at the mighty wreck before me! I thought of the three men he had put out in that early morning fight! Of how, strained and patched and stitched, he had picked up that barrel of flour and carried it in from very pride in his strength! How he had won cheers for his splendid lifting-power at that fire, and now he had come to *this!* He sat there helpless as a child, his only work cutting up scraps of calico for quilts. He was, as he himself said, "an old hulk!" and yet he looked brightly up to me and said: "You remember old lady Brighton, don't you, lass? Unbeliever, poor old thing! Emily and I are going to make a real pretty 'star quilt' and give to her. Star-pattern works up such small pieces, you know! Nothing, most, too small for that, and so bright too!"

It was no use denying it—this wreck *was* dearer—was more valuable to others, *as* a wreck, than it had been in full panoply and strength. He was accepting things—he was conquering himself, and he was "greater than he who taketh a city!"

So there I left him. For background, he had his honest, toilsome, clean-thinking past! His old wife's faithful love was as the blue sky, bowing gently over him. The slow, still sands of Time piling steadily about him, and before him that great, illimitable ocean of Eternity, which will at last receive into its bosom this fine, old hulk!

The Gentleman Who Was Going to Die

The Gentleman Who Was Going to Die

Of course he had a name, and we both knew it, yet we invariably spoke of him not as Clarks nor as Mr. Clarks, but as "the gentleman who was going to die." We must have been a troublesome pair of "little pitchers" to have about, with our widely open ears, in such a place and at such a time; and I remember quite well that our elders were much annoyed when they found that we knew that "the gentleman was going to die."

I was three years older than my companion, and very, very serious; indeed, he was the only child who ever made me enjoy a game of romps. Pretty, golden-haired, laughing little fellow, no one ever resisted him. He passed through his short life a baby Prince Charming, a little, conquering hero.

His father was the Sheriff of the city, and, for the time being, the Sheriff's family lived in that portion of the jail reserved for home life; and my mother was paying a long visit to the Sheriff's wife. That's how it happened that two young children were living within those sullen walls, taking their exercise in its grim corridors and playing their games within the very shadow of the scaffold.

In pleasant weather we used to play out in the jail-yard; it was small, but not so closed in as it now is by the Court-house. At that time the court stood over in the Park, or Public Square, as it was called. Out there we played "escaping prisoner." I, as the Sheriff, had to run down and bring back little Goldy-locks (Charley was his real name) as prisoner. He was very realistic in his struggles for freedom, as certain, big, blue marks on my arms used to testify; but whenever he saw them he would put penitent little lips to them and tell me reassuringly not to mind, "cause he would play Sheriff to-morrow and I cud 'scape," in which case I knew he would have nearly pounded the life out of me, so I very much preferred to keep my part of Sheriff.

In other weather, and it was mostly "other" weather, we sought the corridors of the jail. The dwelling-rooms were small and crowded, and, besides, the big people were all the time "don'ting" us—"Don't do this" and "don't do that"—so Charley would rumple his curls with a small, impatient hand, look very cross for a moment, then come and whisper, "Let's go to jail," and straight we went in search of the turnkey, who was Charley's uncle as well as slave, and he would put a key into a great lock and we would push at the big, heavy door. Then in we would tumble, and the door would be closed behind us, unless some of the prisoners' cells were open. In that case the turnkey remained inside the corridor with us, but that was unusual.

The first thing we always did was to run to each cell and peer in to see if any one was lying down. No one had ever made the suggestion to us, but of our own accord we had made it a point of honor never to make a noise there if we found any one who remained on his cot after our arrival. Generally every one sprang up and came to the barred doors to greet us, always with nice words, sometimes with very gentle ones. Often they would lay wagers on the result of our games. We used to play "tag" and "blind man's buff," and we played "puss-in-the-corner" by counting every other cell door a corner.

That corridor had two great attractions for us. One was that the late afternoon sunlight fell through the barred window at its end. The other was that "the gentleman who was going to die" had his cell there, and Charley loved him, while I was filled with terror, dread and pity by the sight of him. There were three long, troubled years between Goldy-locks and me, and I knew dreadful things about Charley's friend, things I dared not tell him.

With every human being in or about the jail the boy was the pet, the favorite with one single exception—"the gentleman who was going to die." He favored me almost to the point of adoration, no one guessing why till he himself explained the mystery.

My heavy, brown braids and solemn, saucer eyes seemed to blind him utterly to the touching beauty of Goldy-locks, and when we stood before his cell door while he told wonderful stories, selected especially to suit the boy's taste, his eyes were on my face, his fingers held a bit of my little, white apron, or he drew one of my long braids between the crossed bars of his door and stroked and kissed it. Though at that time I loved the stories and liked him, I could never quite make up my mind to kiss him, and Charley used to be angry about it, and once he told me "I wasn't dratefu', not one we'est bit on carf, not to kiss dear 'Mr. No. 3'"; that's what we always called him before we knew he was going to die—three being the number of the cell in which he was confined.

When I first learned that Mr. Clarks was going to surely die, on a certain positively named day, I was utterly amazed to find that, instead of being frightened and sorry and sending for doctors, everybody seemed to be pleased—that is, everybody out in the streets and in the stores and markets, and being an active, "two-legged why," I sought information and obtained it in that form known to man as "straight." He to whom I had applied was a very young man, who knew no reason why a child should be spared such horrible knowledge, and so, with brutal frankness and ample detail, he had explained exactly why Charles Clarks was going to die.

It was the first tale of crime that had been poured into my shrinking, childish ears, and it gave me a distinct shock. I was quite feverish by evening and had to have wet cloths applied to my burning head, while during the night I cried out again and again about the "lightning and the knife," and the next day found me white and miserable, with only one strong wish, and that was to keep away from "the gentleman who was going to die."

It was so hard to associate the man with the bright, blue eyes, the manly voice, the gentle hands—ugh! those hands!—with that wretch who had hacked the life out of a fellow-creature for a sum of money. It seems curious, but the actual taking of the man's life had not near the power to torture and torment me that this complete ignoring of a certain sentiment had. The victim had been a fellow-countryman who was unutterably homesick, and whose joy was boundless when he met a friend from the dear, old English home. I would moan aloud when I thought of the awful surprise and horror the man must have felt when he received the first knife-thrust in his breast from the hand of a brother-Englishman in a strange land. Then the shocking details that followed the death! The crime was committed at night during a memorable storm. The body lay upon a railroad bridge; the victim's identity must be destroyed! The murderer attempted to remove the head; he had but his big clasp-knife, and it was not strong and sharp enough to sever the bone in the neck. He would have to leave the bridge to find a stone to serve as a hammer in this frightful deed! But in that inky darkness how was he to find his way back? He could only wait for the dazzling glare of God's great flashlight, the lightning; and so with unshaken nerves, bit by bit he worked his unhallowed will. He found the stone and crammed it into his pocket (the other held the dead man's effects); the knife he carried between his teeth. The mighty wind so tore at him that on the bridge he had to creep upon his hands and knees. He hacked off the head and tied it in a silk neckerchief, and no man knows more unto this day. The stream was dragged, trees chopped down, open ground carefully plowed, all in vain. The head was never found.

With devilish mirth the murderer would sometimes offer to find the head. "Leave me my hands free and send but two men, your bravest, strongest picked men to guard me, and I will send you back the head—I swear it!" he would say; and to the Sheriff's smiling question, "And you? You say 'send,' not 'bring.' Would you not bring the head back?" he would reply, "Oh, I say now, you don't think me quite a fool, do you?" and though he would laugh heartily enough, there would be a quickening of his breath and a hot spark away back in his eye not very pleasant nor by any means reassuring to the man who was responsible for his safe keeping.

Two days after I had picked this bitter fruit from the tree of knowledge I found myself, under the orders of my yellow-haired, little tyrant, slowly and unwillingly entering the jail corridor again. Holding me by the hand, he pulled me past the turnkey and made straight for the dreaded cell. At our entrance various greetings reached us: "Hello, babies!" "How are you, little ones?" "Come up here, youngster, where I can see you!" while the man with the cough called out, "Sissy, come here and I'll give you half of my licorice!"

But I stood in silence, my eyes fixed upon the stone pavement, while my little companion, trembling with excitement, put his first, troubled, anxious question: " Dear Mr. No. 3, are you truly a-goin' to die ?"

The silence that came upon the occupants of the other cells at this question might have been the silence of death. Mr. No. 3 made a little sound like that the grown-ups make sometimes, and afterward say : " Oh, I had a stitch in my side ! " and then he answered, " Why—er—yes, my boy—we are all going to die— you know that ! "

Charley's delicate brows knit themselves together distressfully as he slowly murmured, " Yes, evweybody. My papa is the biggest mans in this town and he's goin' to die, the whole of him, only, only—" suddenly his brow cleared and he hurried on—"only he and us allis jus' goin' to die som'time, not a 'xac'ly day to know about. Are you goin' to die in free weeks ? Please don't ! "

Instead of answering directly, he turned to me with, " What's the matter, little lass ? Why don't you speak ; are you sick, child ? "

I thought of the lightning and the knife, and truly I was sick, but I could not speak; I only slipped my hand through one of the openings in the door and clung silently to a bar. Charley turned and looked at me, and said in his important, little way : " I dess she's got the aches in her head ag'in ! But please, Mr. No. 3, what's a-goin' to be the matter wiv you, if you are goin' to die ? "

And then No. 3 laughed a laugh that made me cold, and said, " Well, your father and some of his friends think I am going to die of a throat trouble, but I'll bet five dollars they are mistaken!" and then again he spoke quietly to me: " What is it, child; why are you so pale?"

He gently took my little hand in his. I gave a scream and tore it so roughly from him that it was badly cut in passing the bars. I raised my face—and I suppose some of my loathing fear and horror must have been written there, for never shall I forget that next moment! He was looking down straight into my eyes, when suddenly his own flared wide open, then as quickly narrowing to the merest, glittering slit, he gave the most awful oath I ever heard, and angrily muttered: " They have told her! She knows all, this little child! Oh, how could they do it! How could they do it! What cruel beasts men are!" And then rang through the building one great, appalling cry, like that of some wild beast in pain and rage. At that cry all was wild commotion. The turnkey struck out one peal from the alarm bell, and was tearing open the great lock of the main door. No. 3 suddenly clenched his soft, white hand and drove it with all his force against the iron bars. The blood seemed to leap from his gashed wrist and hand and fall in streams down into his sleeve. He seized the bars of his door and shook them as another man might have shaken a wooden lattice. The turnkey was at the cell; was in; there was a scuffle of feet. The heavy, wordless breathing of desperate men, two clear, cold-sounding clicks, and No. 3, with white, drawn face, lifted his manacled hands high above his head to strike a killing blow, stopped suddenly, and pitched forward on his cot, face downward, and as the turnkey hurried us out of the corridor I heard that dreadful sound that wrings with pain all there is of womanhood in any female thing, whether she be seventy or seven years old—the sound of a strong man's sobs.

The next morning at breakfast we learned that we were all invited to visit Charley's grandmother in the country, and his father was going to send us in a day or two.

Little Goldy-locks raised surprised eyes and remarked, "I fought we always made hot visits to drandma's?"

Now his adoring grandparent would undoubtedly have admitted that Charley did make his visits warm for her, but what he meant was that their visits had always been paid at the farm in hot weather. Getting no answer, he went on: "What's the use, there ain't anything grode yet?"

"Oh, yes," said his mother, "there's grass and flowers, and perhaps the peach trees will be in blossom."

There was a little silence, then lifting his dear eyes to his father's face, he asked, "Papa, will it be free weeks while we's away?" No answer came; then again, "Papa, I love drandma very much, but—but—the gentleman might die while we's all away, and I'd be so sorry, papa." His little head drooped, and the tears ran fast down his cheeks. My mother was nearest to him, and she took him in her arms and stroked his curly hair while exchanging looks with his mother, and his father raised up his six-feet-two of height and simply fled in silence from the sight of that innocent, childish grief.

But I was happy—happy at the thought of getting away from the place where "the gentleman was going to die." Charley was anxious to go to his friend at once; he said he had "free whole things to tell him, most 'ticular."

So he dragged me off with him, and lo! there sat a strange man inside the corridor and right beside No. 3's door. We would not go in while he was there, so we went out and down to the yard together, talking excitedly, and wondering who the strange man was.

There we heard, as we managed to hear everything, that Mr. No. 3 was going to be put into another cell. Back we went to the corridor to ask about that, and there sat the strange man. Then Charley grew quite angry, and, turning to his uncle, said, "Why don't you give that man a cell and not have 'im settin' roun' in the way all the time?"

And, under cover of the shouts of laughter of the prisoners, we retired a second time, defeated. It was late in the afternoon when we made our third attempt to see "the gentleman who was going to die." We had little hope of success, but suddenly, to Charley's great joy, we saw in a big, square cell, the strange man, with some others, trying the bars with hammers, and we slipped past and begged the turnkey to let us into our corridor quick. He smiled and said, "All right, chicks; I guess this is your last chance at No. 3 without the watch. Even his wife won't see him alone next time she comes."

As we tumbled past the big door the sunlight burst out from behind a cloud. Charley gave a shout, and crying, "You can't catch me 'fore I touch the sunshine," bounded away toward the window. He was well ahead, but I started after him, and almost in the same instant I saw him slip and throw out his arms. He did not trip; he slid exactly as though he had been on the ice, and then fell heavily, face down on the stone floor. There were many exclamations of pity as I rushed to him, crying, "Oh, Charley, darling! are you hurt very badly?"

I stooped over to help him, but instead of rising at once, he turned slowly over and sat for a moment on the floor and said, "What made me slip?" I only repeated, "Are you hurt, dear?" and though his lips quivered piteously, he bravely answered, "No; only some places smart some, that's all."

And all the time that I was lifting him to his feet and noting the steady spread of that cruel mark on his face, I was conscious, coldly conscious, that at No. 3's door I had seen no face, from No. 3's cell I had heard no voice. Once again Charley lifted up his puzzled eyes to me and said, "What made me slip?" and putting his arm around my waist to steady himself, he raised his right foot, and resting it on his left knee he looked at the sole of his little slipper and it was wet.

I leaned over and passed my forefinger across it to make sure, then without thought drew my finger down my white apron and left a long red smear. The man in the cell nearest us groaned. I gasped, "Blood!" and Charley hid his face in my garments and trembled like a leaf. Holding him tight with my both arms I looked behind me, and there across the gray, stone floor, slow, sluggish and sinister, there crept a narrow, dark-red stream, silent, so stealthily silent, and yet in that instant's pause I seemed to understand the excitement it would presently create.

A moment we stood a pair of terror-shaken children; then holding Charley in my arms I rushed madly for the corridor door. The turnkey, peacefully reading his paper, heard us coming and said, "Not through already?"

Then as he turned his head his face went white as he finished with, "What is it?"

I laid my hand upon the smear on my white apron and gasped, "Blood!"

He was unlocking the door as he said, "Where?"

I pointed a flickering forefinger at the slow stream and answered, "No. 3," and as he rushed past us he cried, "I knew it! God! I knew it!"

Before he reached the cell door he called back to me, "Ring the bell—hard—hard!"

I pulled the big bell and then pandemonium broke loose. The narrow, silent, little stream was beginning to show its power. I hurried down the back stairs and put Charley in the hands of a housemaid, who cared for his hurts and put him in bed and sat by him, while I, making myself as small as possible, crept back through the jail corridors because I could not keep away.

All was excitement. The wildest rumors had already reached the private part of the building. No one noticed me. I crept up the stairs, and for a little while dared go no farther. While I waited there people went and came. One man, tall and bearded, with a black box or case like a big book in his hand, I recognized as a doctor.

I softly followed the path that all had taken to No. 3's corridor. I stood still in the doorway for the very excellent reason that I had lost all power of movement. Once glance told me the little, red stream I had seen creeping from beneath the door of cell No. 3 was gone, the stones being still wet from their washing, while a second one told me more washing would be required presently. At the far end of the hall, on the floor beneath the window, was stretched the form of "the gentleman who was going to die." His lower limbs were fully clothed, but from the upper part of his body they had cut the clothing and he was nude. At his feet knelt two men who used all their strength in trying to hold him down. At each shoulder knelt a man who grasped him by wrist and forearm, and with dripping brows bent over him with the same purpose in view. The doctor, on his knees, was leaning across him, while a step away Charley's mother stood with her face covered with both hands, and each and every one had fearsome, bright red stains upon them. A sudden thought came piercing through my dulled brain, a thought that brought me near to my undoing. I said, "Can this be justice! Are they going to repeat here in this very jail the awful act committed on the railroad bridge that stormy night?" I am certain that a roll of thunder at that moment would have killed me outright. As it was, my eyes closed, and I had a faint feeling of wonder as to whether I was going to fall asleep. Fortunately, I heard certain words that dismissed the grotesque fear and gave me back a little strength; words of advice, of stern command, of argument, and once sobbing words of entreaty. But through them almost continuously there rose a sound of horror. I thought then, and I have never changed the thought since, that it was like the fierce growling and snapping of a mad dog.

Encouraged by the words I had heard from all, I opened my eyes. At that same instant the doctor, with a gesture of despair, raised himself, and I was looking full into the awful face of Charles Clarks, murderer and would-be suicide. He had attacked the citadel of his life at his throat. With an almost ludicrously inadequate weapon he had done terrific work, and had almost carried out his purpose. He lay there now, that thing to marvel at—a fighting Englishman brought to bay. And I, a little, shivering child, stood there witness to a savage struggle, awful beyond description, and gathered up and let go of my apron with the regularity of a mechanical toy, while in a whisper I said, and said, and said, perhaps a thousand times—I do not know—" Oh, our Father! Oh, our Father! Oh, our Father!" And one man with a gashed throat and veins nearly empty battled madly for death against six strong fellow-creatures who fought with equal desperation to save him! "Oh, our Father!" What a smile when he heard the doctor say, " Chloroform could not be brought before the light had gone." The doctor saw, and his face grew like stone, and he said, " He shall be held! The wounds must be stitched at once!"

He bent again to his attempted work, and instantly the ghastly head was jerked this way and that, and there rose again the growling and the snapping. The doctor raised his head and said coldly, "Mrs. B——, you must save us; you must hold his head!"

A cry rang through the jail, and in an instant No. 3 was still. She said, " I can't! I can't!"

The doctor insisted. " Your husband will be a ruined man if this prisoner dies before his time. Kneel there!"

She knelt. No. 3 said, in his strange, whistling sort of voice, "You have been good to me, but do this thing and I will curse you here and from the Hell I'm going to."

The doctor commanded, " Put one hand here, the other there, and hold firmly with all your strength!"

Then as five held him the sewing was accomplished, and I turned to fly from the hurt I thought the needle might give him, and stumbled to my mother's bed. She was not there; all thought I was safe by little Charley, and I fell upon my knees and went right on muttering "Oh, our Father!" until I began to feel very light, and then to float, float, and the next I knew it was morning and I was very sick, but a maid told me that "the gentleman who was going to die" was not dead yet.

The attempted suicide caused the greatest confusion and excitement both inside and outside the jail. People were coming and going at all hours, and the grown-ups were more than ever anxious to get us away to the country. Mrs. B—— would not leave her husband at such a time, so my mother was to take us both the next day.

Little Goldy-locks never gave up his intention of seeing and saying good-bye to the gentleman who was trying so hard to die (in his own way). So through tears and kisses, and by bringing to bear all his graces of body and manner, the little fellow won his way, and just before leaving mother led us (dressed for our journey) to the cell, and the uncle-turnkey let us in. A nurse crossly admonished us all not to talk too much, and then we were standing by the bed. At the first sight of the ghastly face—the grimly bandaged throat and jaws and brow—the little lad gave a cry of terror. But when Mr. No. 3 said softly, "Charley!" he ran and swarmed up the bed with legs and arms, crying, "Oh, dear, dear Mr. No. 3! I fought it wasn't you!

Who hurted you? My papa will find out and he will put the man in a cell, and we won't never go and see 'im, never!"

Then being told he must not talk so loud and that he must hurry, he said very earnestly, as he brought from his pocket a small, red wad, "Here, Mr. No. 3, here's my wed stocking; I got it my ownse'f for you. If your froat should get sore, like you said, you dess put it on at night and you'll come all well in the morning—dess like I did."

A smile parted the man's white lips as he said, "Thank you, my boy—I may try it—though I suppose —hemp would suit—my case—better than wool."

All this time his eyes had gone past Charley and were on me. My mother noticed it, and now he hurriedly whispered "Good-bye," and as Charley was taken down he motioned to have me lifted up into his place. Then in a whispering voice he said to my mother, "You think—it strange—eh, well!—it's because she is —so wonderfully like—my child—my only one—my Annie. It's marvelous—the likeness. It's not that they both—have that same—surprising length of hair —the same wide, gray-blue eyes—the same tricks—of manner and movement—even to that habit of standing —with hands behind the back—gently pulling at the two great braids. But it's the voice. I've been ready —to swear at times—that my wife—had broken her vow—and had brought—Annie to see me. And though I starve—for the sight of her—until at times I'm almost mad—I'd kill my wife—if she brought—the child here—to know my shame. And this little one—is so like her—so like and yet so different—for Annie loves me—while this child——"

I felt my face flame with hot blood, for my mother did not know I had been told of the murder, and I was frightened, but he went on gently, "Ah, well, there is no reason why this one should—love me—a stranger."

The nurse exclaimed, "Too much talk."

Mother moved toward the door, but Charley broke from her and once more climbed up on the bed. "I have dess one 'ticular thing to say, dess one!" he pleaded, and he stooped to whisper to the sick man, "Dear, dear Mr. No. 3—try to get well—and—and—I know you don't like the preacher man, but I know my own night 'prays' my ownse'f, and when I say 'my soul to keep' I'll say 'your soul to keep,' too, every time!"

And Clarks groaned, "For God's sake take him away!" and Goldy-locks put his clean, sweet, little pink lips lovingly to those sin-stained, fever-parched ones and said "Good-bye, good-bye!" and slid down and ran and hid his tears in the folds of my mother's dress.

I moved to leave the bed, but he laid a detaining hand lightly upon me. I shivered, and looking up I met his gaze and was held by it. It was pleading—commanding, almost compelling. I understood him perfectly, and I tried hard to break away from that controlling glance, but all in vain, until a dimness came across his eyes and slow tears gathered there. Then I wrenched my eyes from his and hung my head and whispered, "Good-bye." As my mother called me I slid off the bed to go to her, but the hoarse whisper came, "Little torment!" and I stopped. Again, "Dear, little torment!" and foolishly I looked at him, and for the last time our struggle was renewed, and now I had to resist not only his pleading, but that of something within me that said, "Think of his little daughter who cannot tell him good-bye, and kiss him for her sake." Almost I yielded—and then—the homesick friend, the bridge, the knife, and I threw back my head violently and exclaimed, "No! No! I can't! but——" and I laid my little hand against his lips. He took it gently, gently, and sighing heavily he kissed it, palm and back, and every dimple, including the tiny one in my wrist, and every finger-tip, and then said under his breath, as it were, "Good-bye, little maid who knows her own mind," and as the key was turning in the lock after we had gone from the cell we heard him give a husky laugh and say, "She's got a will—it's stronger than mine—for, mind you, she never kissed me!"

And that was our last sight of "the gentleman who was going to die," because that bright day, when Charley and I were out making the acquaintance of a very remarkable calf—remarkable because its forequarters were mild and gentle, while its hindquarters stung like an adder—and we were about to play marketing, and we both had a desire to purchase the forequarters of the calf, and as we never quarreled we drew lots for choice, while the calf slowly chewed up our market basket—and at that very moment, in the city, Goldy-locks' beloved "Mr. No. 3" was heading a procession to the scaffold with many a jest about the "blue funk" he said the men were in about him. He remarked their pale faces and trembling hands, and actually encouraged and advised them, himself directing the proper placing of the fatal knot. Then with alert, springy step, bright eye and cheerful voice he mounted the scaffold, stepped with quick obedience upon the trap, and was hurled out of this world into—what?

White and cold and silent his wife removed her coffined dead, and when we returned "the gentleman who was going to die" had died. He was gone, and his cell and corridor knew him no more.

Old Myra's Waiting

Old Myra's Waiting

Was she mad? I do not know. I only know that she was old, oh! very old, and had known such sorrows as break the heart and blast the intellect of many of her sex. So old, so fragile — so poor — with a wit like polished steel and a tongue like an adder. I was her one friend in the world and was as helpless as herself. We each earned our own living—that was the one experience we had in common. Save for that, there was a whole world between us. She stood wavering and unstrung at one end of life — I stood quivering and tense at the other end. She had known it all, all, and only wished to sleep, to forget—I knew nothing, and only longed to learn, to feel, to know.

The first time I saw her she stood on the bank of the lake, a little, swaying, black-robed, figure, facing a blinding gale. The wild wind tore her pitifully thin shawl from her shoulders and sent it whirling down the lonely street. I set my long, young legs in motion and ran it down, and returning, put it about her sharp, old shoulders.

She gave me one piercing glance from the blackest eyes I ever saw. Her dry, pale lips drew back across her rather long, narrow teeth in a sort of smile, and she said: "My dear, you are a wonder; few young people condescend to run like that, particularly for the old. I thank you!"

She turned her face again to the lake. Though I found it hard to keep my position, she somehow managed to maintain hers, frail as she was. I was puzzled—why was she standing there, so thinly clad? I hesitated a moment, then I said as respectfully as I could:

"Madame—could you not go into one of those houses, or home, perhaps, and let me wait here for your message or—or friend, and then come and tell you?"

She turned her sharp eyes upon my face, and exclaimed: "God bless my soul! the girl means a kindness to me!" and she laughed a shrill, thin peal of mocking laughter that made me hot with shame and anger too, and I turned away with a brief "I beg your pardon;" but she could be quick if she was old, and her claw-like hand was on my wrist in a moment, and her sharp voice reached me through the wind: "I can't, my dear, I can't leave now! You see my treasures are out there, and if they should be given up, I want to be at hand. Go home! my dear—go home, where people are not old and mad, and do not wait for the sea to give up their dead," and turned again to face the gale, while I flew like the wind from her strange presence.

Some weeks passed before I saw her again, and then, as it happened, was able to do her a second small service. The day was wet and windy, the streets muddy. I was hurrying down Bank street and was about to cross an alley-way, which opens on that street, when I heard a little cry behind me, and there rolled past my feet a very neatly done up, small package, with a large seal on it in red wax. It stopped in the middle of the alley directly in front of an advancing dray-horse. I snatched it up and sprang across to the sidewalk, where I waited for the owner, who came hurrying across with anxious face and outstretched hands; and behold! there was my strange, old lady again.

She seized the package, and examining it carefully, she muttered, more to herself than to me: "I hope it's safe, a fortune blowing about the muddy streets like that!"

My face must have been an expressive one; at all events she read it like a book, and went on rather sneeringly:

"Oh, I'm not mad; at least, not *now!* This does not belong to me; it would not be a fortune if it did; it's lace—old, rare and very valuable! Had it been ruined? Oh, it makes me quite faint to think of such a chance! I am really very grateful to you, my child!"

She spoke her thanks so gracefully that I felt myself grow pink with pleasure.

We walked side by side a little way, when she said: "My dear, I'm not a stupid woman, but I can't quite make you out. Your speech and bearing says one thing, but your being out so much, quite unattended, says another. Oh! I've seen you many times since that day at the lake. Then, your clothes—they are too good for poverty; but you wear the same things too often to have generous and well-to-do parents. No, I don't quite understand."

We were right at the door of the old "Academy" then, and I stopped, saying: "I go in here; there is a rehearsal; I am a member of the company."

I never saw such fire as could leap into those fierce, old eyes of hers—at that moment they fairly blazed.

"Here, you!—you with that clean, honest, young face! For fifty years I've had a curse, hot and burning in my heart, for theatres and all connected with them!"

Then angrily shaking her forefinger at me, she cried:

"You run up your flag, girl!—your flag of red and black, of paint and dye!—that honest craft may know there's a pirate in these waters!" and, dragging her veil across her face, she left me standing there, divided between the desire to laugh and the desire to cry. A pirate? I was such a harmless, well-meaning, little pirate that even had I shown the flag, and blackened my lashes and rouged my cheeks, I doubt if I should have created a very great panic in the Cleveland shipping—and so, at last, the laugh won; and between laughs I said aloud: "I am a pirate! I am a pirate!" And so a member of the company found me, and paused and looked me gravely over, and, wagging his head desperately, said: "It seems incredible, such meanness in one so young, but you will bear in mind I *saw* this myself—a girl of sixteen, who knows a good story, takes herself out into a cold, damp hall, and tells this story to herself, and laughs and laughs all to herself, and then wipes her mouth and goes in seriously and sadly to join her defrauded brother and sister artistes. Clara, I wouldn't have believed it of you!"

I had to tell him what I was really laughing at.

"Good Lord!" he said, "that was old Mrs. Worden. Do you mean to tell me you don't know her? She's a terror, is old Myra! She used to carry this town in her pocket. She was young then, and rich, and they do say Myra was a beauty. Hard to believe that, isn't it?"

"I don't think so," I replied. "Her features are really perfect. Her eyes must have been very fine; her hair black, and her figure very graceful."

"Perhaps," he yawned, "but she has the sharpest tongue and the longest memory in Cleveland. How she does lash some of our public men! You know the rector of Christ Church, the party who abuses theatres so often? Well, one day there was a race between the ancient Myra and the long-winded Reverend. She was overhauling him fast, and he knew it. These doors stood open—theatre doors. He was between the devil and the deep sea, and—well, quite properly, he chose the deep sea, and slid in here, and behind that billboard. Had he only known it, he need not have gone behind that board for shelter, for nothing on earth could induce the ancient dame to enter the door of a theatre; so he would have been safe had he merely stepped inside. As soon as she had passed, he tried to slip out unnoticed, but *I* was on the spot, I am proud to say, when I was least wanted, and, lifting my hat, I informed him that if he wanted seats he would find the box-office at the head of the stairs. He *glared* at me, and then I offered to run up and get him a programme of the evening's performance, but he snorted something about 'mistaking the entrance,' and got away. Well," my companion added, with a self-satisfied look, "if there is anyone in town who has *not* heard of that chase and escape, it's not my fault."

"But why," I asked, "does Mrs. Worden dislike theatres so greatly?"

"My dear girl," replied my friend Lewis, "I just love to instill knowledge into your hungry, young mind, but fifty cents are always full fifty cents to me, and if I stand here stuffing you with valuable information, I shall be late to rehersal, and fifty cents forfeit will be torn from my unwilling pocket-book. So *en avant*," and we both turned our faces stageward.

The next day was very stormy and bitter cold. My mother insisted upon my wrapping her shawl about me as an extra protection, but I had not gone more than a block or two before I was in trouble. The wind tore at me, the small pins could not stand the strain, they gave way, open went the shawl. The wind caught it, and slapped my face with it, and flung it flapping noisily through the air. I grabbed for it, jumped up at it, waltzed around and tried to catch it; but truth to tell that shawl could be found most any place in the street except on my shoulders. While I was laboring like a ship in a high sea, I heard some one knocking on a window pane, and just as I began thinking I should have to scud under bare poles for home, the knocking was repeated so very loudly that I looked up, and, to my astonishment, there stood Mrs. Worden! I was amazed, because I had supposed the house to be unoccupied. The lower part was so, but at the upper window she was standing and making signs for me to cross over to her. Still wrestling madly with the shawl, I plunged over. The old lady opened the front door, showing an empty and bare hall, and holding tightly to the door itself, to keep from being blown backward, she motioned with her head for me to come in. I obeyed, and stood leaning against the unfriendly-looking wall, trying to regain my breath. Mrs. Worden smiled sardonically at me, and remarked:

"I don't think you will get to your precious rehearsal to-day at that rate of speed. I've been watching you prancing about with that shawl, and I've brought you down this."

She held out to me a shawl pin. As I took it, I found it was yet warm from the hand of its maker since it was formed of a stout darning needle with a ball of red sealing wax for a head. She had seen my trouble and had hastily made this shawl-pin especially for me. I was surprised beyond speech for a moment, and she mistook my silence, for she began to jeer."

"Oh, use it, use it! If you can keep that shawl about you it may save you from a sickness. Then you can hide the pin from the sight of those lords and ladies at your great, fine theatre. They are so artistic, I fear its roughness and lack of finish might jar upon them."

But I shook my head, and, smiling broadly at her, I said:

"It's no use, Mrs. Worden, you can never frighten me again. I know you now, and you are good and kind."

A sort of wonder came upon her: "Good God!" she cried. "You must be madder than I am!" then she turned her eyes to the rough, gray lake spreading far before us, and on her face there grew the look it wore the first time I saw her. She spoke out quite distinctly, but apparently not to me:

"I wonder if you hear?" she said. "I wonder?" You used to call me good and kind, aye, and dear, but that's five and forty years ago, a weary time my prettys! Perhaps the sign is coming soon—"

I stood a moment, then I laid my hand gently on her arm and said: "See, now, how safe the shawl is; I thank you very much, and I shall get to the rehearsal in time, after all." She looked a bit bewildered for a moment, then she asked: "Shall you be long to-day?"

"Oh, no," I answered, "I shall be through very early."

"Then suppose you stop in here a bit and have a cup of coffee?"

I accepted the invitation eagerly, and, as I ran down the steps, she called to me: "You, girl, who won't be frightened any more, I may be out when you come; see, here's where you'll find the key, and just go right up to the front room and wait for me."

I nodded, and started again, but once more through the wind came her shrill call: "You, girl, don't you touch the fire, if you have to wait; mind now, don't touch it; I attend to that myself."

The door slammed shut, and I was slammed down the windy street, but in considerable comfort, now that the thick shawl was fastened securely about me. I have seen—owned very handsome shawl pins since then—some double, with connecting chains of silver or of gold, and cunningly decorated by the goldsmith's skill, but none ever gave me better service than did that darning needle with its head of wax, made beautiful in my eyes by the kindly thought that prompted its creation. I was really quite excited at the prospect of seeing her at home. She was an acquired taste. I had found her bitter at first, but now there was a faint hint of sweetness rising above the bitterness, and I liked it. I hurried to keep my appointment, and as I approached I was struck by the resemblance the house bore to the woman who lived in it. Both were so old, so gaunt, so lonely, and, above all, so frail. Surely, I thought, that trembling, old, frame shell of a house cannot be safe in any great off-lake gale. And when I first entered it and mounted its sagging, old stairs I was really frightened when it jarred at every quick movement and shook in each blast of wind.

Mrs. Worden was out when I arrived, and so I entered gladly the front room she had indicated, for, silly as it sounds, I must admit I am, and always have been, afraid of an empty house. I went in and closed the door.

Now, the French say, when colors do not agree 'that they swear at each other,' but never, surely, did inanimate things swell to such a storm of profanity as did the furnishings of this room. The floor was bare, the boards were narrow and warped and hungry-looking. Guiltless of stain or paint, they had been scrubbed to a creamy whiteness, which somehow gave the whole floor a peculiarly frigid, unfriendly look. It had a Pharisaical air, as though it were thanking its maker "that it was not as other floors." Then, exactly opposite the door, there hung upon the glaring, whitewashed wall, in a magnificent frame, a life-sized, full-length portrait in oil, of a charming girl of about ten years. The "swearing" here was almost audible. The windows, ill-fitting and rattling in their cases, looked out directly upon the lake. The bedstead had been a grand affair in its long-passed day, but now, stripped of all its luxurious hangings, it stretched its thin, old posts up, only to meet the skeleton of its former canopy, while the silken spread of patch-work, of a brain-destroying intricacy of pattern, was worn clear through in places, so that the cotton wadding showed plainly. As I turned slowly around, I found another great portrait. This time it was a boy who smiled happily at me from the canvas; such a handsome, manly little chap, for all his absurd dress. One only smiled with him, not at him. I was very much impressed, for I had only been in two houses where there were family portraits, and I knew they meant a great expenditure. And then, ignorant as I was of such matters, I felt sure these portraits were the work of some great artist, and I was right, for later on I learned they had been painted by the most famous artist of his time.

Two small tables, a bureau, a few chairs, all of the commonest, and a small corner cupboard, completed the furniture of this odd room. Oh, yes; I must not omit the screen, then a very unusual object, a tall, narrow, three-panelled screen, which played an important part in its owner's daily life. And the fire! Thank Heaven, I thought, for one thing, that did not look cold. I think there was about one scant quart of fire, and, as I threw off my shawl, I started to put on some coal, when suddenly I remembered that injunction, 'You girl! don't touch the fire!' and I stayed my hand, but when I looked into the box and saw there just four pieces of coal, and so suspiciously exact in size one to the other, and leaning at the end of the box a hammer, my heart melted with pity; I began to understand. With a sigh I left the fire, precious but inadequate, and turned to study the painted pair. The boy, swarthy, smiling, happy, won your love at once; but the girl's blonde, young arrogance slightly repelled. The portrait, considered as a picture, was quite lovely. The dainty figure, in the soft, yellowish-pink gown, stood out well from the olives and dull greens of the brocaded curtain behind her. On the table lay her great hat, while just slipping from her shoulder was the black velvet pelisse which, by contrast, brought out so beautifully the milky whiteness of her childish neck. The features, the lift of the head, the thin, slightly shrewish, delicate lips were all wonderfully like Mrs. Worden. But the color scheme was wrong. This handsome, overbearing child was blonde as she could be, while the boy, with but one feature of her face, her piercing eyes, was surely darker than she had ever been. So while I stood before the girl and thought how clever had been the artist, who had painted the boy with his hand upon his dog's head—while in the girl's hand he had placed a broken necklace—in these bits of detail, I thought he has given his idea of their character, and just then I heard Mrs. Worden approaching.

Like many people who live much alone, she had the habit of talking to herself—she was talking then. I heard her say, "That's fifteen years ago, you fool! yes, all of that. Now, what the devil did I do it for?"

I felt quite certain she was referring to the invitation she had given to me, and I shook with laughter. When she opened the door, her eyes were snapping viciously and her brows were brought together in an inky frown; only her hair was white, her brows were black as they had ever been, but when she saw me standing, my hands behind me, evidently studying the portrait, the frown unknit itself, her eyes softened, and when I asked: "Who are they, the handsome girl and the laughing, little man?" she answered proudly: "They are my treasures, my man-child Philip, and my Edith, gift-of-God; because of whom I have not cursed Him long ago and died."

At the words, "my treasures," I suddenly recalled her speech at the lake, and instinctively my eyes turned towards it. She caught the look, and, going to the window, she went on: "My treasures, precious beyond rubies, they lie out there now; I watch them and wait for the sign."

Then, pointing with her long, bony finger, she said: "You see that dark line out there on the water; no, no, the darker, purplish one? That's where they lie. Yes, yes, my prettys, I know, I know! but it's weary waiting, dearies; weary, weary!"

Her voice died away so drearily that I felt the tears rising in my eyes. A movement of mine made her turn to me. She put her hand up and passed it across her brow and eyes once or twice, and then, quite naturally, she went on: "I was wondering, when I came in, what I asked you here for."

I interrupted to say: "I think it was to give me pleasure." "No," she answered, "it wasn't that. I know now. I thought I'd like to hear some one talk again."

I felt a bit flattered at that, but she finished with: "I haven't heard any one talk at home since my parrot died."

Down sat my vanity, flat. The old lady had taken off her bonnet, and, as she motioned me to a chair, she said, musingly: "I never can quite remember whether I learned to swear from the parrot, or the parrot learned from me."

She heaved a sigh and proceeded to prepare the tray for our coffee. As she moved about she continued her remarks: "Yes, we did a fairish bit of swearing between us, Poll and I; her name, by the way, was not Poll, but Sally, and, of course, I suppose some one must have taught her to do it, but it was delicious to hear the 'bloomin'' cussing she would give to any one who called her Sarah. Yes, all things considered, there was in the past considerable profanity in this room."

And I, glancing at the splendid frame against the whitewashed wall, recklessly made answer: "And it is not absolutely absent at this moment."

Her bright, old eye glanced from wall to frame, then back to me, her quick comprehension making my unfinished thought her finished one in an instant. She wagged her head and said: "That's not bad, you girl," then, with somewhat unnerving loudness, she went on: "She's young and green, oh! but upon my soul, she's not a fool." Then addressing me again: "So you know some French sayings, do you? Not many though, I think; but look, you, young ears are sharp, and you should have been here before the hangings of my bed fell to bits. They were of brocatelle and lined with silk, and they cursed that whitewashed wall so venomously, had you been here in the bed, you'd not have slept one wink, unless your soul's already gray instead of white," and she laughed that odd, stinging laughter that was so like the crackling of thin ice upon a wintry day.

While she had talked and laughed and nodded, she had prepared her coffee, and we seated ourselves at either side of the little table, she taking care to sit facing the tossing lake.

Oh, that tray! It really seemed as though the things thereon must come to blows, so fiercely did they contradict each other. The coffee pot of make and material precisely like those good "Bridgets" purchase for the use of honest "Patricks." The knives and forks—they appeared a bit later—were of that brand which always makes you wish that you were dead, they make of life a thing so hideous. While cheek by jowl with these rough things stood a few pieces of old porcelain, deserving, each one of them, a satin-lined box to rest in. And to keep them in countenance, there were four spoons of silver, paper-thin, initials and dates quite worn away, and all a trifle bent and dented in spite of the owner's care of them; while the linen, I could have cried over that eye-destroying mass of delicate darning. Truly, there were places in my napkin where the darning had itself been darned again. But the coffee, like the fire, which had been increased by the addition of one small cube of coal, was inadequate in quantity, but the qaulity? oh, well, it was perfection, that's all; absolute perfection.

I tasted it and smiled, and sighed. She understood, and snapped her old eyes at me approvingly, and *she* tasted and sighed, and then she slowly said: "Whenever I drink good coffee I always rejoice that God created it. It would have been an infernal shame had it been invented by some fool man!"

I laughed aloud—I always did, I'm sorry to confess—whenever she swore, she did it in such an impersonal way, never, never in anger, never, even when she was busily engaged in flaying alive some victim of her memory and her tongue. She generally swore to herself, and nearly always when in a reflective mood. When I laughed, she gave me a glance and asked quickly: "What is it, eh? Did I swear? Well, don't you do it, that's all. But Lord! you won't have to live fifteen or twenty years alone with a 'cussing' parrot, as I did. For some time after Sally died I used to say 'damnation.' Oh, I don't say it now; don't open your eyes any wider, you'll meet with an accident. But, you see, for nearly twenty years that bird told me twice a day that her coffee was 'too damnation hot,' and after she was gone I had to say it now and then to break the silence."

As she talked she fidgeted uneasily with her spoon and cup; at last she broke out with: "My dear, I asked you just to have coffee with me, but now—well, to tell you the truth—I am quite faint. I breakfast at half-past six, that I may have the strong morning light for my work, and somehow I feel a bit exhausted to-day, and—and I'd like my dinner now, if you can pardon an old woman's offence against all conventionalities, and stay and dine with me!"

Could I have known, I would have taken the coffee only and denied my hunger; but I knew nothing, and cheerfully consented to dine with her. I wondered where her kitchen was, and, supposing she would be some time preparing the simplest meal, I looked about for something to help me pass away the time. There was no paper, and but one book in the room, a family bible that might have been bound in a pair of old boots—its leather was so browned with age, so worn, so scruffed it looked. I went over to take it up, when my hostess, with distinct satisfaction in her voice, announced, "Dinner!" All my life long my generally-absent appetite has been pursued like an "*ignus fatuus*" by those near to me, but this time my appetite met its match; old Myra's saw mine and went it about four better. The knives and forks had now appeared, simply as a mockery, I believe. Lying on a plate were four biscuits, or, as we called them then, crackers. They belonged to that branch of the cracker family known as "soda"—soda crackers, and while I looked on in stupid wonder, she carefully opened a handsomely-cut, glass box, with a silver lid, which, beyond the shadow of a doubt, had been her powder-box in days gone by, and delicately lifted out *four little, thin scraps* of smoked beef—four crackers and those scraps of beef—no more, no less—and we fell to and "dined" upon them. But when I saw her trying not to eat too eagerly, I had a lump in my throat bigger than our whole dinner. No wonder her weight was less than a pound for each year of her weary life. I wished I could gather her up in my arms and kiss the fierceness out of her eyes and promise her fire enough for real comfort, and coffee, and food—real food—that would not make the promise of nourishment to the eye to break it to the stomach. My thoughts were broken by "You, girl! is there anything the matter with your dinner?"

"Nothing in the world," I cried, "but I was not very hungry, and, in fact, I do want to get back to my coffee."

"Well," she answered, "I must say you eat fairer than ever Sally did, for, I give you my word, for years on end that parrot cheated me out of at least half a cracker every day of her life, and yet, my dear, when she died she was as thin as I am."

When I was about leaving her, she said to me: "You, girl, I like you! You are queer. You are uneven, and you make me guess. You know more and you know less than most girls of your age, and, thank God, you don't giggle! You may come again." She paused and looked at me with a deprecating expression, and finished almost meekly: "That is, if you care to share your spare time with me."

I told her, and I told her truly, how glad I should be to come. How glad I was to live in Lake street too, and so near to her, and then, rather shyly, I added: "I think, if you will let me, I will tell you my name, Mrs. Worden—and I mentioned it.

She was looking out at the dreary lake again, and, without withdrawing her eyes, she made answer: "H'm'm! Clara, eh? Cla—ra, Claire—Clarice—that's a fool name, Clarice? but Clara—that's light, illustrious, clear, bright! My dear, I'm glad you are named Clara. It's a good name. I hope it may fit you as well as mine has fitted me. My French mother meant to call me Marie, which is, you know, a form of Mary—'Star of the Sea,' and he who did the sprinkling and the crossing and the rest was deaf, and he named me Myra —'she who weeps.' Good God! Good God! Have I not been well named? 'She who weeps.' The tears are all gone from the eyes, now, and they are dry enough, but hot, my dearies—so very hot! Internal, cruel tears that ooze slowly, like drops of thin, old blood, still fall from my heart, my dearies, while I wait and wait. Aye, it was before the altar, and with the sign of the sacred cross, and the touch of the holy-water on my brow, that he baptized me 'Myra'—'she who weeps!'"

I stole out of the room, where well-bred hunger showed its teeth so plainly, and softly closed the door, leaving her in the gathering darkness, a ghost talking to other ghosts, from whom she was separated by the thinnest, frailest shell of mortality I ever saw.

And so we went our ways, and did the work that fell to us. Some nights I pranced cheerily about the stage in country dances, and made announcements anent that carriage that always seemed to be waiting for some one in the old plays, particularly the comedies. "My Lord, the carriage waits!" It is a famous line, a short one, I know, but powerful enough to produce temporary paralysis of the limbs and complete dumbness, for the moment, in strong and lusty youths and maidens. Well, I was on most friendly terms with that line, and some nights said nothing more, while on other nights I went on and played really first-class parts, that being the manner in which we used to work our way upward from the very bottom, and felt no shame in it either; but *nous avons changés tout cela.*

While I was thus bobbing up and down upon the restless waters of my profession, my strange "old lady," who had grown to be my friend, was sitting "like a gray, old Fate, toiling, toiling, weaving" the fairy-like stitches that made whole again the torn or injured among rare and precious laces. Her knowledge of them was wonderful, her love for them almost tender. She would shake her head and croon over them, when they were, in her words, "badly hurt." The day she came nearest to loving me was the day I said I thought laces were the poetry of a woman's wardrobe. "Aye, aye," she answered, "that's a good word and well said, girl Clara. It's strange that, without teaching or information, your keen instinct guides you to the *real* beauties of life as surely as the sense of smell guides a young hound on the trail. There's nothing made by the hand of poverty that is so beautiful as lace; so delicate yet so strong. Ah! girl Clara, some day, may you see a bit of Venetian 'point,' 'round point,' but if you do, you'll smash a commandment, mark my words!"

Laces were sent to her from distant cities, and the package I had caught up from under the horses' feet came, as did many others, from the then greatest merchant of New York. She had received much work from the South, but the war deprived her of that. So she went on cutting her expenses down to meet her earnings, starving quite slowly and making her moan to no man.

One day I paid a long-promised, much-dreaded visit to a young friend of mine. We had made our first appearance in the ballet together, the same night, the same play, and she was still in the ballet. She was the young person who gave me the decorated fly-trap for a Christmas gift. Somehow that remarkable selection of a gift always seems to have had something to do with her remaining so many years the chief ornament of that ballet. I had gone with her from rehearsal to her boarding-house. Now, there are boarding-houses and boarding-houses, but this was just a boarding-house. The sadly experienced ones will understand exactly what I mean. The happy, inexperienced ones may just skip the sentence.

Rehearsal had been long, so we were late for dinner and we seated ourselves at the long, narrow, untidy, unfriendly-looking table, with heavy forebodings. Everything seemed to have been devoured by the boarders before us, except the pickles. They alone coldly and sourly faced us. But when the slatternly waitress came in, I asked myself why, oh, why had I come at all? A slattern with a cheerful face is hard to bear, but a slattern who sulks is more than even a boarder should be asked to endure. I saw my friend, whose name was Mary, quail as this fell creature looked insolently at her; but before our doom was sealed the landlady passed through the room. Now, Mary always said that had she been alone that incident would have passed for nothing, and that she would have dined on pickles and cold water, or not dined at all, but I was there, and Mrs. Bulkley knew of me, and being stricken for the moment with madness, saw in me a possible boarder, therefore she paused and greeted me, and rather unnecessarily explained that the dinner was all gone, but added that she reckoned they could scrape something together for us. And Mary rather ungratefully whispered, " she was used to living on scrapings now." While we waited, the sulky slattern, regardless of our presence, proceeded with her duties, snatching everything from the table, except the shame-faced cover and the pickles.

Presently Mrs. Bulkley appeared, and our dinner materialized in the form of liver and bacon and warmed potatoes, a vulgar dish, but, being freshly cooked, a welcome one to two tired and hungry girls. Had it not been for the table-cover we might have been quite happy, but the sins of the boarders against it had been many, and as they had not yet been washed away, they were not pleasant to look upon.

Just as we were being served, Mary remarked that she had "seen that awful, old Mrs. Worden giving a gentleman fits in the street that morning, and that two other gentlemen were waiting for him, and they had laughed at him," and she ended by asking me "had I ever seen her?"

"Oh, yes," I answered, "I saw her in her room yesterday."

"What?" cried Mrs. Bulkley, dropping the spoon noisily from her hand. "What's that? You saw Mrs. Worden in her room, her own room where she lives? Oh, nonsense, you don't mean our Mrs. Worden! She hasn't had a soul inside that room since old poll Sal died."

I explained that my Mrs. Worden was "Myra," owner of Sally, living at number so-and-so Lake street, mender of laces, etc., and then Mrs. Bulkley dropped herself, a friendly chair catching her; then she said:

"Well, I'm dummed!" Then she took off her spectacles and wiped them on a corner of the table-cover, which made them worse, as I knew it would, and she took them off again and wiped them on a grimy handkerchief, and put them on, and looked hard at me and said: "She had you in her room, and you a theatre-girl? Well, then, she's breaking up at last. Well! Well!"

She leaned her head upon her ugly, old hand, and I asked:

"Do you know her personally?"

"Do I know her!" she snapped out at me. "Don't she come here every once in a while? and sometimes she takes tea with me!"

"Yes," faintly murmured Mary, "and when she comes, a clean cloth goes on the table, and every boarder in the house who has 'a past,' keeps in his or her own room."

I smiled comprehendingly, while Mrs. Bulkley went on: "Do I know her? good Lord! haven't I known her since I was a green girl in my early 'teens?"

I was startled. Looking at her foxy, false front, her steel-bowed spectacles, her leathery skin, and the small framed platter she wore on her chest as a breast-pin, it was so hard to believe she had ever had any ''teens' at all!

"Yes," she went on, "I know her, as my mother before me did. She worked for Mrs. Worden for more than eighteen years, and now she's breaking up.

Here, Hannah, make me some tea! You, oh, well, yes —you may make enough for us three, and bring it here. I feel all tuckered out."

And the old body did look worried and anxious. I was surprised, and I was grateful for her interest in Mrs. Worden, for whom I now had a real affection as well as a great pity.

"Oh, Mrs. Bulkley!" I cried, "don't be uneasy; Mrs. Worden seems quite as well as usual. She works as hard as ever, too, and she is very kind to me."

"There!" exclaimed Mrs. Bulkley, " that settles it! Myra Worden kind to anyone in her eighty-third year? She's breaking; she'll get the sign she's been waiting for so long pretty soon, I reckon, poor thing!"

I simply could not help putting the question: "Do you know, Mrs. Bulkley, why Mrs. Worden hates theatres so bitterly?"

"Do I know, my Suz!—Oh, here's the tea, and glad I am for it!"

The tea was good, and I saw by the gratified astonishment of Mary's face that it was a treat. When the "Busy B" (as Mrs. Bulkley was generally called behind her back) had had her first cup, as a pick-me-up —a sort of green-tea cocktail—she felt better. She loosened her specs and let them slide well down her nose, so she could look at me over their tops; she planted her black alpaca elbow on the dingy table, and unlimbered, ready for conversation, while, for the first time in my life, I recognized these signs in a landlady without instantly taking flight. "Why," she began, "it was like this: Right from the first every one said she'd throwed herself away when she took up with that great, big, pink-and-white chuckle-head, Phil Worden. But she was just plumb crazy in love with him. I suppose he must have cared a little for her at first, but mother always said he just married her out of vanity—like gals do sometimes—she being the biggest catch in town. Good looks, and money and family the hull thing! Well, anyway, he was a foolin' her, or thought he was, before they was married a year. She knew of it in no time. Mother thought there'd be an awful rumpus, but Mrs. Worden shut herself up all afternoon alone, and walked and walked, but when supper-time come she just met him as kind and as sweet! Oh! Myra used to be sweet enough in them days, and she just talked and laughed, and he looked like a great school-boy expecting a good trouncing. Well, that blowed over, but Myra Worden was always on the watch, I reckon, after that. Mother used to say he was, somehow, afraid of her. She loved books—good Lord! the books she had; lots of 'em writ in French, too; and she first off tried to talk of 'em to him, same as to visitors, and he didn't know a thing about 'em. Then she tried to read them to him, and mother said she didn't know which one she felt the sorriest for, him or her; him trying to keep awake, or her trying to hide her disappointment. Well, by-and-by, she gives it all up, and, if you'll believe me, that educated, fine-minded woman just took to readin' out loud to him a nasty, low-down paper—I can't just call its name now, but all about cock-fights—oh, yes! they had dog-fights and cock-fights in my time, my dear—and ring fights, and horse-races, and he'd just drink it all in, every word. She was fond of music, and he couldn't tell one tune from another, he said; but that was just an excuse, because he hated to have to sit and listen to decent music. Common fiddling suited him well enough. He was almost stupid in behavior or sulky-like in company —proper company; but if, by chance, he was left home at night and his wife was out, he'd carry on with the servants, and sing songs, and play tricks with the cards, and imitate things—pigs gruntin' and corks poppin', and that like, until you'd laugh to split. In that sort of way, mother used to say, she thought he felt afraid of his wife's finding out his real disposition, and she—why, she just followed him about with them black eyes of hers, and fair worshipped him. She was nigh tickled to death when her girl baby came into the world; yellow-headed like him. She was only like him in color, however, for of all the domineerin' little hectoring brats I ever saw! Well, as I was saying, Mrs. Worden was the law of this town then, and it was card parties and coach parties and sleigh parties and lake moonlight parties, accordin' to the time a year, and dinners and suppers and 'routs' —that's what they called 'em then, I remember—and people used to come from other places and they'd stay a week at a time, and them weeks was Phil Worden's picnics, his two-forty-on-a-plank days, I tell you. Now, I never see nobody so dead crazy about theatres as Miss Worden was. Whenever a company came here she had the first box, and every night of her life, unless she gave a 'rout,' she was in that old theatre. Yes, I know it, an alley now, and only a few low variety shows go there, and no women ever enters its doors, but then it was, my Suz! it just was a fine theatre. Well, Phil was fond of the show, too, and she was awful proud of that, and it was 'my Philip is so fond of the play,' and 'Mr. Worden will be at the theatre whether or no—' Poor soul! it was so seldom they liked the same things, but Lord! even then she was deceivin' herself. He didn't care for no play; he just went for them dances they used to have between the acts, and the slack wire performers and that like; but he knew every man and woman behind the scenes, and knocked about with them in the daytime, and I don't mean no slurs against you two girls now, but in them days actors was a rather common lot. The men nearly all drank too much, and, what's worse, some of the women did, too; and well, one crowd came here for a long stay, and Phil Worden was just cock of the walk with them, and before long there was talk about one special female. She wasn't even a leadin' actor among 'em, just a brazen hussy who put paint an inch thick on her cheeks and daubed her mouth with a dye thing they called 'vinegar rouge,' because it wouldn't come off easy, and she was poorer than Job, and all at once she had beaver bonnets and velvet pelisses and feathers and long gloves and a muff big enough for a base drum. And because the woman was drunk oftener and oftener, and in her cups was a noisy and quarrelsome jade who would fight her best friend, and talked everything right out, all Cleveland began to wink and nod and say Phil Worden. Well, of course, Myra must have suspected, but never one cross word did she give him, nor show him the frown mother said she had on pretty often them days when he was away. But, one day, in he comes, near supper time—even Mrs. Worden took her dinner at two o'clock them times, and people said it was all airs to have dinner so sinful late. Well, in he comes, all bunged up, a sight to see! His eye was all swelled up, and there was blood smears on his face, and his lip was hurt. Mother happened to be right there when he came in, and she looked first thing at Mrs. Worden, and she said her eyes flashed fire. She stood right in her tracks, looking in her husband's face, and her hands were shut tight, and at last she said, and her voice cut like a knife: *'How did you get your hurt, Mr. Worden?'* and he looked away across the room and mumbled something about 'sky-larking with a fellow who was drunk and hit harder than he knew,' and she, as white as death and as cold as ice, said: 'You lie, you coward! You lie! Not even a drunken man fights with his nails! A woman did that work for you—'

and she threw open the door and pointed for him to go, but in came the two children in their gowns, with the nurse behind, to tell them both good night. Her arm fell like a log, and she made a spring and caught him by the shoulder and turned him so the young ones couldn't see his face, and pushed him towards her dressin'-room and said all in one moment, 'poor daddy! has got hurted, so mammy must tell you good night alone this time,' and when she kissed them the boy said, 'Sall 'ou tiss him hurt, mammy?' and she says: 'God knows! God knows!' and mother said she got away with the dresses she was carryin' and only knows that Myra nursed him faithfully till he was able to face the world again, and for her pay, one week later he left her, to follow the third-rate actress, who beat him in her drunken frenzies—like the dog he was. He left a letter for her. My mother stood, shaking like a leaf with fright, but Mrs. Worden stood like a rock and read it all out loud: 'How he was not her equal, how she had been too generous and too kind,' and then mother said he quite worked up there, and blamed her hard for not flying out at him when he done wrong. He said he could have stood it better if she had abused him, but she held her tongue or only spoke gently to him, and at the very end that's what he said, 'You should have lashed me, I could have understood that, but your tongue was not sharp enough,' and then she stopped, my mother said, and then she read that line again, 'your tongue was not sharp enough,' and then, says she, with blazing eyes and white lips, 'By God! no other man shall make that complaint of me! I'll sharpen my tongue like a serpent's, and adder's poison shall lurk under my lips!' and then suddenly she began to laugh and laughed and laughed, and while we all went a running for doctors, she laughed her way into the fever that came nigh to killin' her."

The tears were on my cheeks, and my tea was stone cold, when Mrs. Bulkley paused to refill her exhausted lungs and swallow another bracer. Mary had, meantime, been steadily eating, grinding with the regularity of a machine, swallowing with the satisfaction of a *gourmet*. She had devoured her own share of the meal and was now making predatory attacks upon certain portions belonging by rights to me, and I, believing that the "Busy B" was only getting her second wind and would start again directly, told her in a whisper to go ahead and eat it all, an arrangement satisfactory to us both, since I preferred Mrs. Worden's story to eating, and Mary preferred eating to any story of any woman alive or dead. Mrs. Bulkley was about to resume her narrative, when she paused to shout an order to the cook in the kitchen "not to use none of that *good* butter in no cooking out there," and I actually felt my flesh creep. It was the double shock that told upon the nerves. There was first that awful attack upon poor Lindley Murray, pounding him with negatives, then there were the rending possibilities connected with the butter that *would* be used in the cooking out there. And I was glad that I was not Mary. Mary, hearing that order, had simply let her eyebrows slide up her forehead a bit and then slide down again, while she went on eating. Mrs. Bulkley suddenly remarked: "I see you're crying; well, well, I used to cry about Myra Worden myself, sometimes. But when you get old your tears come harder, like everything else, pretty nigh. I don't know's I exactly sense why you should cry for her losin' that great hulk of a fellow, though."

"Oh!" I cried, "her pride, think of that! To have been abandoned for some great woman, some rare beauty, would have been bad enough, but to have been cast aside for a gross and common thing that cursed and tore him like a beast, and all in the very face of the public! How could she bear it all, poor thing?"

"Well," said Mrs. Bulkley, "she done it somehow. But I must tell you a queer sort of thing about when she was sick—yet it jest shows you what dummed fools women be. Mrs. Worden had the most amazin' head of hair I ever seen in my born days, as black as jet and hangin' to a length I darsen't name, for fear you'd think it lies, and thick! good mercy! Well, she was in for a long sickness, the doctor said, and no nurse could do anything with that mop of hern; and so they ups and cuts it off, and mother cryin' like a baby when they done it. But when she found out herself what they had done to her—good Lord! she give a screech, and wrung her hands and sobbed: 'It was the only thing that Philip ever loved about me. He called it his great, black mantle, and once he wound it round and round and round his strong, white throat, and now *its* gone; thanks to these meddlin' fools, who don't see that I can't die!' and she jest cursed every man and woman in the house, and raved over that hair of hern every hour when she was out of her head—when she was right-minded she never let on she noticed about it. Well, at last she got well, and straight she put on the widow's weeds that she's worn for five and fifty years. Poor soul! she held her head so high and looked so hard right into folks's eyes, they darsen't ask the questions nor make the remarks they'd like to. And she used to spend an awful lot of time and money on the poor—and she jest guarded them children as though they was chuck full of dimonds. But 'twas *then* she began to use the sharp edge of her tongue. She didn't talk *about* folks, she never was one for slander, but the things she'd say *to* 'em was jest awful, and the worst of it all was, that she always told the truth. If she'd jest been abusive and have made up things outen whole cloth, nobody would 'a cared much; but what was it, now, that big lawyer said about her once? Let's see, she had been giving him a hidin' right before folks, and when she was done, he says, 'The woman who is armed with sarcasm and truth is a woman whose tongue is sharp on both edges.' Yes, them's the words.

"But trouble jest follow'd right along after, yes, and pretty close after. 'Mrs. Myra Worden,' that's what her cards said *then;* they used to say Mrs. Philip Worden—but when the black went on the 'Philip' came off. Mother said that she never heard her speak that name but jest once, after the time she stood laughin' like mad over his last letter. Some one told Mrs. Worden that some one else had said that 'she had a tongue like a serpent's,' and mother says her eyes give a flash and she throw'd up her head and she said almost wild-like: 'I swore me an oath and I'm keepin' it. You should have waited; my nails are long now, and sharp; already I have a serpent's tongue. I might yet learn to cuff, and curse and tear you with the rest! Ah! you should have waited, Philip!' My Suz! then came the trouble. Didn't the biggest man, most, we had in town up and blow out his miserable, dishonest, old brains, because he had first lost his own money, and then had thrown away a hull lot of Myra Worden's after it—expectin' to get both back, he said. It was an awful loss. She didn't say anythin', hardly, but she shook her head a bit, while she watched the young ones playing; she only cared for their sakes. Some one said to her, 'Such a disgrace, I do wonder what his family will do?' and she says so quiet-like: 'Get a much larger monument than is usual, and see that it's of whitest Carrara, I suppose. That's what's generally done in such cases.'

"Well, she give up livin' in that house, and give up all the carriages but jest a family affair that the children could be sent about in, and came down to Lake

Street. It was a pretty house, but Lord! not like *her* a bit. And if you'll believe me, that girl, that Edith of hern, cut up more monkey-shines and was madder than a hornet about it. Little Phil thought it was fine; fact was, the little devil was in the lake about half his time, but nobody liked to tell, and everybody knew the dog would take care of him anyhow. They got along all right for a while, she living for the work she could do for the poor and for the love of them children, and they for lessons and fun. My Suz! she had 'em so they could jabber French all the time they was dressin' and until lunch, and then at that meal that Dutch woman she had, great flat-faced, stupid thing, used to pitch in and make 'em eat that meal in Dutch, or German she call'd it—though I vum! I can't see no difference between the two. And dancin' lessons! and, O, Lord! I can't remember half they were studyin' at, and so their mother let 'em have lots of play too. So one day, she'd promised to take 'em to the circus at night, and they were sure the day would be a year long; and some one invited 'em to go out on the lake for a sail, and she ups and says, '*no*.' Well, they was mad; but she was weather-wiser than any woman I ever see, and she said to 'em, 'No, my dearies, its fair now, but its a treacherous fairness. I dare not let you go.' Well, after sulkin' a bit, they asked if they might go and spend the day at Auntie Anna's? She wasn't their true aunt, they jest called her that, and she was nothin' but a slave to 'em, and spoiled 'em—well, don't talk!

'But,' said their mother, 'if you go there to take tea, you will not have time to dress for the circus!' 'Why, then, dress us now; we'll be careful of our things, mammy,' said Edith, 'and then we'll come right from tea, by our ownselves—oh! please, mammy, yes by our ownselves, and we'll stand on the corner over there and wave our hands and handkerchers to you for a sign for you to come to us, and then we'll all go on up town together.' They were jest sot on that plan. They felt it would be so big for them to come alone, those few blocks, and then to stand on the corner and make signs for her to come to them, and seein' as she had already cross'd them once, she consented, and right away they were dressed and started off under the servant's care to their auntie's house for the rest of the day. When they had kissed her good-by about a dozen times—for the way they loved her jest was a caution now, I tell you—little Phil runs back and he up and said, 'Mammy, I'll take care of Edie—she's the biggest, but I'm the strongest, and I'm the nearest to a man, ain't I? So, I'll hold her hand all the way when we're alone, mammy, and I won't let anybody speak to her, 'till you come down to us,' and she kissed him again, and called him, as she often did, her 'man-child,' and away he went after Edie. The next time she saw the poor, little things, Phil was a keepin' his word.

"Mrs. Worden went on with her doin's, whatever they was, and along couple hours later she sees the sky darkenin'. There had been a good many small boats out on the water, and she felt uneasy when she noticed 'twas getting dark. Everythin' along the bank was different then to what it's now, you know. Some of them long slopes was all green and right pretty to sit out on, and lots of people used to walk there and look at the lake and do their sparkin', and sometimes people would crowd the bank to watch a wreck and shout and yell, if any one was saved. Well, as I was sayin', Mrs. Worden she goes to look out, when a girl comes screechin' to her 'that a boat had been capsized, and the folks that had gone out to save the upset people were now in danger from the wind that was blowin', and there was crowds out there watchin' already!' Mrs. Worden wraps herself up in a cloak and goes out, too, to the bank. Lord! Lord! that storm! and the shortness of it. I had a sailor boardin' here then— nasty, drunken brute he was, too—he said somethin' about their having where he come from what was called a 'black squall,' and that that was one. Well, I don't know nothin' about black squalls, but I do know, and you know, and every one else as knows 'Old Erie' at all, knows there ain't no lake on God's earth that's as treacherous or as lightenin' quick in evil-doing, and when Mrs. Worden gets out there, the crowd was already cryin' out, and wringin' hands, and runnin' up and down. And, sure enough, there right close in was a bit of a pleasure boat of some sort, and, oh, dear! I can't tell you no rights or wrongs, I was there too, but when I seen them poor creatures hold out their arms towards us standin' safe on solid ground, I jest sot right down on the bank, for my legs couldn't hold me up. Then a rumor ran through the crowd that there was children on the boat, and one great groan went up, and Mrs. Worden says: 'God pity some poor mother's heart! my own children might have been there, for they begged to go out to-day, but I forbade it,' and right behind her stopped a woman who had come up runnin' like mad, and was movin' her lips and not makin' a single sound, and that woman was Aunt Anna. At that moment a vivid flash of color was seen on the deck, it was a girl's pink dress; next instant the crowd groaned: 'The children, oh! God! see the children! and they are holdin' hands, they look this way!' A man was standin', holdin' a pair of glasses to his eyes, and without a word Mrs. Worden put out her shakin' hand and seized them, while the silent woman, with the ashen grey face, fell down upon her knees and bowed her head behind her. The instant the glass was at her eyes Mrs. Worden stopped shakin'. She stood solid as a rock and she jest said: 'Oh! Mother of God!' and there she stood, and it was only a moment or two after that, oh! well, there was awful screechin' from the women and some groans from the men, and it was all over. I looked at her. She took the glass from her eyes, and holdin' it in her hand a minute, she stood looking down at it, then she gave a kind of start-like, and she holds it out to the man, and she said slowly, each word kind of by itself, 'I thank you, sir, it is a good glass,' and she turned and walked a step or two, and then without a sound, fell all her length, upon the ground. They carried her to her home, but Aunt Anna was taken to another house and cared for, and there she told how she had not been strong enough to refuse them, when they had entreated, and the people who invited them were old friends of hers, and would, she knew, be very careful ; but where she took on the worst, was when she told about how the dog had to be tied, to keep him from following them. The ladies feared he might jump into the water and get in the boat again and spoil their dresses; and he fought like mad to get loose, and howled and barked his voice clean away. And I havn't no doubt but he'd a saved one of 'em, for he was that strong, and a regular water-dog, and he'd brought the boy out against his will more than once, when people had sent him after Phil just for fun. Well, Aunt Anna was afraid of her life to meet Mrs. Worden, but she needn't have been, for she hardly noticed her when she did see her. The doctors that come that time didn't like her doin's at all. She never cried a minute. That's the truth, and she had seen her own and only children go to the bottom of the lake hand in hand. People that went there cried; the help just cried buckets full, and she looked at 'em, and one day she said : ' I wonder how they do it ? I can't!' and the doctor, once he got kind of mad-like, and he says: ' Bend, woman, bend, or you're bound to break ! Do you think you have the strength to bear this blow as

you bore the other one?' but she only answered
calmly: 'I am what I am! I did not make myself.'
When he left he felt all upsot and he was cross as a
bear with a sore head, and he said when Aunt Anna
came up to ask about her, 'She will cry, or die, or go
mad; and the last looks the likeliest to me,' and off
he went. The minister he tried what he could do.
He was a pudgy, kind-hearted man, and he had young
children of his own, and he tried to talk resignation
and that sort of thing, and she jest said to him when
he got good and through, 'Has *your* house been made
desolate to you in one hour?' and he jest burst right
out crying, and he says, 'Ah! you poor woman, how
can you bear it?' and she jumped from her chair and
lifted up her face, and beating on her breast with both
her clinched fists, she almost screamed out: 'Bear it?
Bear it? Why I—' she stopped right in a minute and
she sat down and said, 'You will pardon me, won't
you? But, see now, you have little ones, yours, your
own blood in their veins, and you can imagine, can't
you, the hunger, the agony of hunger I suffer for a
sight of my little ones' faces? I could wait a thousand
years if only I could see them then, but they're out
there!' waving her hand toward the lake. 'Never,
never, shall I see them again!' and he, poor, old man,
he jest sobbed and said: 'Never, till the sea gives up
its dead!' At them words she gave a great cry—that's
the way the minister put it—she gave a great cry and
she said: 'My God! My God! I had forgotten—when

the sea gives up its dead, and His words stand firmer than the everlasting hills!' She threw herself upon her knees, and holding up her hands she cried out loud, 'Lord, thou hast sent my soul down into hell, but for Thy great words, will I praise Thee forever!' She turned and kissed the minister's hand and blessed him for reminding her. 'They are truthful children, and have long memories,' she said, 'and when the sea gives up its dead, they will give the promised sign, and I will join them, and we will all go on together. 'So I will watch and wait, just watch and wait for my dear ones' sign!' And that was full fifty years ago, for I was but eighteen then, and Myra Worden has watched at that lake's side faithful ever since; though from that day people have called her mad, and I suppose she *is*, poor soul."

I bowed my head upon my hands; dully I heard Mrs. Bulkley going on about some bank's failure, something about a fire that had followed close upon the failure, and the word ruin, many times repeated, but my real attention was fixed upon a picture that rose before me. I saw, as plainly as I ever saw anything in my life, a great, level plain, and far away against the angry sunset sky, a line of low unwooded hills encircled it. It was unspeakably dreary—no trees, no water, no rise and fall, dip or break in the monotonous, dead level of the ground. Far away to the left, in the growing darkness, I saw the towers and cupolas of a fair, white city, and from its distant gates a path was worn across the dismal plain—a path so faint, so narrow, it could only have been made by one lone traveler's feet. At the very farthest end, and on either side, there were faint outlines as of fallen bodies, and there were broken urns, and jars, and some withered garlands; but for all its greater length, it was narrow, faint and bare. And while I looked, suddenly, at its opposite end, that nearest to the hills, there appeared the figure of that traveler whose weary feet had worn that piteous path. Behind her, the fair, white city; before her, the bleak and savage hills. The tall figure, in its sombre garments, seemed the very spirit of desolation. The face was turned away from me, but there was that in the figure which made my heart leap up in quick recognition, and then, so truly as you live, *then* I heard a voice, clear and distinct, but seemingly very, very far away, and it said: "I am Myra, 'she who weeps!'"

I gave a start so violent that I turned my tea-cup completely over, and, putting it hastily to rights again, saw Mrs. Bulkley looking her grimy handkerchief over carefully to find a promising bit to rub her glasses with. Her false front was much awry, and her small eyes were red, and she was finishing, as she had begun, with the assertion that "Mrs. Worden was breaking up, no doubt of that, since she had taken up with a theatre-girl, of all people on the footstool, well! well!"

I thanked the "Busy B" for her tea and her information, and I greatly fear I proved an unsatisfactory confidant for Mary, who dearly loved plenty of "oh's!"

and "ah's!" and "did you ever's?" while she poured forth tales of the numbers of magnificent male creatures who madly pursued her through life, she always baffling them, however. By the way, she must have kept up her habit of baffling the magnificent ones, because she eventually married a baker with a veritable low-comedy name, by the side of which " Bowersocks," would look grave and dignified.

The pain I felt in hearing Mrs. Worden coarsely and disrespectfully spoken of opened my eyes to the extent of the veneration and affection I had grown to feel for her. That creature in whom the world saw a desolate woman, whose haughty, old head was held high, and whose piercing, hawk's eye spied out its weakness, but in whom I saw the wearily faithful, old watcher, by the restless lake, waiting through the long years, always " waiting for the sign." To me, her sorrows had made her sacred.

I had never seen any creature who seemed so absolutely bloodless as did old Mrs. Worden, and no matter how often I might meet her, the moment my eye took in the waxen pallor of her face, I experienced an uncanny feeling of familiarity. I would ask myself, " Of whom does she remind me?" knowing all the time that I had never seen any one who resembled her in the slightest degree.

But one day as she sat, as ever, facing the lake, with her eyes cast down upon her cup, the cold, dull light falling upon the clear-cut features of her wax-white face, turning it into a veritable mask of death, I looked steadily at the hollow of her temples—not the faintest pulsation there. I gazed steadily at her throat—not a pulse-beat could I see, though I knew my own full throat would throb and swell at times as though it had an independent existence. As I looked, I thought, if she should run a needle deep into her finger I believe nothing would follow its withdrawal, and so, like a flash, it leaped into my mind who she was like. The very counterpart of old King Duncan! He of the mighty tragedy—the victim of that woman who raved in her crime-haunted sleep; not of pity at his "taking off," not of remorse, but only of that stupendous surprise: "Who would have thought the old man had so much blood in him!"

The good, old man with the wool-white locks, and the saintly soul housed in the parchment-like body—yes! like this he looked. Yet her dagger thrust had been followed by a rush of royal blood that not only "laced" all his followers and "pooled" about his body, but stained her hand with a stain too deep for an ocean's waves to wash away.

Never since have I read or thought of Duncan without seeing Mrs. Worden's features beneath the golden round of sovereignty. All the life, the strength, the spirit she had left, was gathered up into the fire of her eyes, and when the ashes of her lids covered their glow, her face was as the face of Duncan, dead. Were Mrs. Worden living now, she would probably be called a "mind reader." Then many people declared her to be clairvoyant. Be that as it may, she had, beyond doubt, a wonderful power of reading or guessing other people's thoughts, a power which added greatly to the terror with which she inspired some of her townsmen whose thoughts were not always of a quality or nature to invite close feminine inspection. As for myself, she had divined my thoughts, time and again, with a calm exactitude that filled me with awe; and that day, while I still gazed at her mask-like face, she raised her eyes, looked steadily into mine a moment, and in an even voice asked: "Well? Whom am I like? The Witch of Endor?" and, without a moment's pause, obediently as a little child, I made answer: "No, ma'am, you are like King Duncan!"

A quick frown knit her black brows. Never since that far-away day of the giving of the shawl-pin, had she, by word or sign, hinted at her knowledge of my being an actress, and I saw the allusion to Macbeth was unwelcome to her. However, she quickly recovered from her annoyance, and, with her usual aptness, asked: "Do you find the likeness purely physical, or do I, like the old soldier king, 'lag superfluous on the stage of life'?"

To which I gaily and gratefully replied: "At all events I shall not, like Mistress Macbeth, try to 'push you from your stool'!"

And her answer, to my annoyance, was: "How—how—is she going to do it?"

She was thinking aloud, but I knew only too well that her question referred to me; and equally well I knew that a bad quarter of an hour was directly before me. Several times the old lady had declared that I was going to make my mark in the world, but she was greatly puzzled, very naturally, to know how I was to do it. She had, therefore, fallen into a way of analyzing my character, before my very face, with positively brutal frankness, and, so far, she had always failed to find out how I was to attain the success she foretold for me.

Really, it seemed a form of vivisection she subjected me to, and I squirmed in unpleasant anticipation when I heard that: "How—how is she going to do it?"

I had no suggestion to offer, so I drank my coffee silently. She studied my face a moment, and then she said: "Yes—yes, you will, I tell you! But, *how!* You are not aggressive enough to win by *force!* Oh, you can fight fast enough, flaring nostrils! but you will always fight on the defensive. You are clever, but you are not clever enough! Intellect isn't going to win for you. How *are* you going to do it? Yet you are to dominate, to have power. I've seen it in the arch of your bared foot, in the unbeautiful square of your shoulders, in the tenacious grasp of your hand. If you had great beauty now—there, don't redden that way: never blush above the eyes, it's not becoming—you are all right; you're straight, and fair, and wholesome. You have enough good looks for men to hang their lies upon, but you have not a world-conquering beauty. Deuce take me, girl, if I can make it!"

While she had been harrying me I had once turned my head to see why the room had darkened so noticeably, and saw a heavy fog was creeping in from the lake, and now that she had come to her "giving it up" place, she turned her eyes slowly toward their usual resting place, the lake, and a quick change came over her. She started a little, then her head drooped slowly until her chin rested on her hand. With unwinking eyes she stared straight ahead of her, while gradually the brightness all died out of them, a slightly distressed raising of her brows threw deep furrows across her forehead, her nostrils were pinched, her thin lips tight pressed, while over all her face grew a look only to be described by one word—a look of woe!

It wrung my heart! I looked and looked at her—the tears rose thick in my eyes, then slowly, slowly I seemed to understand, to *know*, what was grieving her. It was the surrounding fog, silently, steadily, blotting out everything between heaven and earth! Even her longing mother's eyes could not pierce that soft density, could not distinguish the purplish, dark line that, to her belief, marked her darlings' resting place out there in the great lake.

I bore it as long as I could, and then I leant across the tiny table, and, laying my warm hand upon her chill one, I said: "Dear Mrs. Worden, do not grieve, the fog often lifts at sunset. Then, perhaps, you may see the purple line before the night comes on!"

Her eyes came slowly back to mine, she smiled gratefully at me, and then all suddenly the fire flashed into them again. She rose to her feet, her head held high in her imperious way, and cried, triumphantly: "I have it now, girl! You have given me the clue! You will succeed by your power of sympathy! You will not fight the world, you will open your great heart to its sorrows, and the many-headed public will neither growl at nor tear you, but will come at your call, your friend and your defender. When you know you have succeeded, say once to yourself, 'Old Myra saw, old Myra told me true.'"

Then with an indescribably tragic gesture she pressed one hand upon her breast and said: "She who weeps!" while her other hand fell softly upon my head, and she murmured, "Clear, Light, Illustrious!"

Her tone thrilled me, there was such sincerity, such intensity in it. I sat quite silent, but I drew her cold hand down and pressed my cheek against it, and that moment there came a heavy knocking on the lower front door. I sprang up, saying: "Let me go, Mrs. Worden, please!" and, without awaiting permission, went cautiously down the sagging stairs and found a man at the door with the usual sealed package for Mrs. Worden. When the signing for it was all over, I ran back, calling out joyously, "Lace! lace! Mrs. Worden—more lace! You will open it before I go, won't you, so that I may see it?"

Mrs. Worden, meeting my request with, "You girl! When are you going to learn not to prance when you are pleased? Can't you keep your joy out of your legs?" went, all the same, to the other table for scissors to cut the cord and seals at once; for she really enjoyed showing me her precious charges; and I eagerly watched her every movement. The note enclosed she laid aside with a scornful, "Humph! as if I didn't know what to do without their telling me."

Then she unrolled the inner tissue-paper. There were two pieces of lace within. One delicate, oh! as cobweb, I thought, as it lay there in its folds. The other heavier, and a mere scrap.

"Why," said she, taking it up first, "why, this must be, *is* a bit of old Flanders cut-work, but what a scrap! Oh, yes! I see now, it belongs to some collector; it is simply an example of the brave, old work, and I see, girl Clara, it needs two, yes, three, little brides or braces—see where they are broken? I'll have a time, now, to wait for thread to darken to anything like that tone."

And she talked earnestly, almost happily on, about her little tricks and devices for staining threads, etc. Then she laid her hands upon the folded lace: "Ah, I think you're going to have a treat now, this is—" the words died on her lips. From her throat came a sound, strange, startling, neither sob nor groan, and yet like unto both! She held a length of lace between her hands; she swayed slightly back and forth, and turning my frightened eyes upon her face, I thought: "Behold! a miracle!"

From somewhere, somehow, the weary, old heart had forced through her shrunken veins one wave of blood strong enough to mount to her face, where the pained color slowly grew until it burned into two bright spots high upon her cheeks. Those two fierce spots, glowing in the awful pallor of her face, to me were terrible. I ran to her and, throwing my arm about her, lowered her light body into the chair close to the table. Her haughty, old head was bent; one hand still clutched the lace. I did not know what to do, but it hurt me to the heart to see her bow her head. Timidly I laid my hand upon her shoulder. She looked up at me, and in a husky voice she said, with a glance at the lace: "I owned it once, yes, it was mine! I wore it while I was yet a happy bride!"

I shivered and turned away, while I mutely prayed that torturing color might fade from her face before I looked again. I pressed my forehead to the window, I could see nothing; no tree, no building loomed darkly through the fog; I could not even see the pavement below me. So far as sight went, there were but two living creatures in the world, and one of *them* longed to leave it!

I was so lonely and so sad, I turned back again. She sat there still, one hand moving back and forth over the lace. The spots were yet on her cheeks, but they were not so fiercely bright. I did not know her like that. I wish she would accuse me of "prancing," or tell me I "sat down too quickly," or "jumped up" when I rose. I wished she would snap at me—that her dear, old head would lift itself imperiously again. I had not spoken one word since she told me the lace had been hers, and so, still silent, I crossed back to her and sat down at her feet and, hesitatingly, I asked: "Dear Mrs. Worden, is the lace much injured?"

The words acted like magic upon her. In one moment she had the length of lace passing swiftly between her inquiring fingers, and an instant later she gave a cry of anger: "Oh! shame! just look at this—the cruel hurt! and the soil! Why, some vulgar, new, rich, money-flaunting creature owns this dear lace now! She is ignorant and coarse! Oh, I know, girl! Don't you see? She has dragged this delicate web about on the *bottom* of her gown! Its beauty was lost in such a position. It was simply done to show the owner's utter indifference to expense. I'd wager something that it has been sent, now, by some maid or companion to be repaired. Ah! I should have recognized it any way—but look you, here is the proof that it is mine!"

She held out to me a fold of the lace, and careful examination showed where a former tear had been exquisitely repaired. I nodded my head and she went on, her eyes fixed upon the old scar: "As if I could forget! He did that, my fair-haired giant—man without soul—therefore, husband without honor! But, truly, he was good to look upon!"

I moved restlessly; she took no notice; evidently I had ceased to exist for her: "Fickle, changeable as a child, unstable as water! But, he loved me for a little while. He loved me *then*, the night I wore this lace to the *rout*. It was falling full and deep about my bare shoulders, as they rose from the golden yellow of my gown that was brocaded with a scarlet flower. I wore some diamonds and stood with others in my hands, hesitating, when he came in—my Philip—and looked at me reflected in the glass, and, standing behind me, he said, in the great voice I loved: 'Burn my body, but you are a handsome woman, Myra!' and he kissed me on the shoulder. 'Twas like wine taken on a cold day; I felt it mounting to my brain! We were at Christmas-tide, and a bough of holly was hanging above the dressing table. He broke a bunch of its scarlet berries and dark, bright leaves, and, with a great jewel, fastened it here, in the lace at my bosom. His fingers were clumsy and the leaves were sharp as needles, and so my lace was torn—but what cared I? The sharp leaf-points wounded my neck, too, and drew more than one drop of blood, but had they come straight from the heart, I would still have worn the ornament his hand had placed. My Philip! so much I loved him—loved him! Bibber of wine and companion of harlots; fair, like a God, yet without soul; so, being soulless, why should he be cursed for riotously living in the sunlight, and for following in the train of the scarlet woman—with the laughter of fools ringing in his ears! The lace is here, the smooth, white shoulders are shrivelled and bent, the black crown of hair he loved is gone, he is gone, only the lace and my memory are left!"

I drew softly away from her. I felt as guilty in listening to her self-communing as I could have felt had I opened and read one of her letters. I took my cloak, and as I drew it on, I heard her low voice saying: "You said my tongue was not sharp enough, Philip; that was because I loved you! *Her* tongue was sharp, she cursed and flouted you, and stung and maddened, and tossed you a favor as a bone is tossed to a dog! She was not even beautiful, your frail one, but she knew well the ways that lead down to darkness and to death! She led, steeped in vice and reeling with wine, and you followed because you were without soul, my Philip!"

I crept out of the door and left the bowed, weary, old woman patiently examining the torn meshes of two webs. One her web of lace, the other her web of life. And as I stole through the chilly, gaunt, old house not one of its faint voices—and it had many—whispered to me: "It is nearly over—a little while and you will come no more! A little while and she will have gone, and there will be no one, and nothing here only the old, old house, and we, its voices!"

Some very busy days followed—long rehearsals every morning, and a new part, of greater or lesser length, every night; and it must have been a fortnight later when, being out of the bill, I put a bit of work in my pocket, took a book in my hand, and thus prepared for finding my old friend either in or out, started to make her a visit.

As I approached her door, I heard her talking, and said to myself, she must be over by the fire-place, her voice is so indistinct.

I tapped, but received no answer. Just then there came a pause in the talk within, and I tapped again; this time more loudly, but, to my surprise, I received no invitation to enter, though the talking was resumed in another moment.

I felt somewhat hurt, and turned to go away, but something restrained me, and I thought I would first make *quite sure* that she knew of my presence, I would knock loudly. As I raised my hand to do so, I heard a groan. That was enough for me; I waited no longer for permission, but opened the door and stepped in, and there amazement held me motionless; I no not know how long, for this room, whose orderliness had always been of that precise and rigid kind suggesting daily measurements with a foot-rule, was now in complete confusion. Chairs out of place, garments here and there, and the usually spotless hearth a mass of gray ashes and fallen black cinders.

And that small, rumpled heap of clothing at the foot of the bed, with white hair tossed and tangled—was that—could that be my Mrs. Worden?—she whose habits of neatness and purity were carried to the extremities; she who on a bitter winter morning, as on every other morning, sought such cramped privacy as her gaunt, old screen could secure for her, in the farthest, bleakest corner of her room, and there, with unskimped thoroughness, went through with the same process of grooming she had indulged in sixty years before, when she had had her maids to help her, after which she put herself into a sort of bolster case, with a hole in the far end for the passage of her head—and in this blue linen bag she became her own house maid, and when the toilet of the room was finished to the points of its very fingers she again retired to the privacy of her screen and finally emerged "clothed and in her right mind," as she used to say, when she appeared in her worn, old black gown, her black silk apron, her snow-white collar and small cuffs, and her bit of white tulle, by way of cap, upon her satin-smooth hair—and was this she, was this her room?

Suddenly Mrs. Worden drew down the arm which had been resting across her face, and, looking at me, exclaimed: "Oh, Betty, you are so late! Is breakfast ready now? My head aches, Betty; you never kept me waiting so long before!"

She rolled her head from side to side, and moaned a little, and while I threw off my wraps I recalled, with a heavy heart, the words of Mrs. Bulkley: "She's breakin' up; old Myra Worden is breakin' fast."

I hastened to reduce the room to something like order, to mend the fire and prepare some tea and rather doubtful toast, and when I had placed her in her chair and her eyes took in the familiar picture of the lake, they cleared perceptibly. She nodded her head and murmured: "Yes, my dearies, yes! I'm waiting for the sign, you won't be long now! no, not long, not long!"

I came to her, then, with the tea and the toast, and was delighted when she called me "you girl" again, and hoped she would scold me about the fire I had made, but she scolded me no more forever.

She had asked so many times for breakfast, yet now she could not eat one morsel, but she drank her tea like one famishing. While I arranged her bed, she babbled on, and most of the time she talked to her children. Once, however, she declared that if Sally stole another cracker she would throw her from the window, and vowed no one in town would be fool enough to pick her and her vocabulary up.

When I was smoothing her white hair into something like its usual order, one lock escaped my fingers and fell forward on her chest. She saw it and cried out: "They have cut it off, oh, curse them! curse them! Betty, do you see? Its gone, and—" she paused, looking curiously at the thin, glittering strand of hair—"and, Betty, either I've gone mad or it's quite white! Oh, Betty, I *can't* understand!"

And so, as Betty—some long-dead Betty from her past—I put the suffering woman back into her great skeleton of a bed, and smoothed her brow and wet her lips times uncountable, wondering at the heat in her dry, parchment-like skin, while I tried to decide what ought to be done in this emergency.

I felt that a doctor should be summoned, but I stood in absolute awe of her will, her commands, and I knew her fixed determination never to have a physician's care. She held "she *could* not die, no matter what her ailments, until she had 'the sign,' and that when 'the sign' had once been given no power on earth could keep her here."

So I dared not summon proper help; my next thought had been, naturally enough, of Mrs. Bulkley, the only friend of the old days left to her, but as fate would have it, Mrs. Bulkley was absent from the city on business that would detain her two or three days. Had I not heard my friend Mary rejoicing the night before over the very "high Jinks" the boarders were hoping to enjoy during that absence?

Then indeed my spirits sank, and I could only sit there and watch over her until she became calmer, and then I thought I would slip out and tell my landlady and get her to advise me what to do. And so the hours passed slowly by, and I looked them in the face with young, impatient eyes, and never noted their dread solemnity. For all my anxiety for the woman who was "breakin' fast," I had no faintest suspicion that she was *already broken*—that each time the clock struck off the afternoon hours—the four, or five, or six—it was, for the ancient woman in her gaunt, old bed, the *last time*.

To know that we are doing a thing for the *last* time

lends a touching grace to even the commonest act; but I was blind with that black density of blindness that can come only upon the very young, and therefore the very ignorant, and I only waited for the chance to slip away and ask for help for her.

She had been quiet for some time, and I softly rose and tried to leave the room, but she stopped me. "Do not go, girl Clara," she calmly said, and I, rejoiced, went back to her. She was quite reasonable again, expressed a small want or two, wished to be lifted higher that she might see the lake better; and when all had been accomplished, she asked me if I would stay the night with her. Then, with great diffidence, I told her I thought she should have a doctor first; she raised her hand and looked at me with such imperious fire in her black, old eyes that I silenced myself and stood quite meekly before her, while in a few sharp words she disposed of the "doctor" question.

"Pray, what was wrong any way? She supposed she had wandered a little in her speech. Well, what of it? All Cleveland called her mad. I must have heard that often enough? Why, then, a doctor to-day in special? As for Mrs. Bulkley, if she or any one else entered this room, she would find strength to put her on the proper side of the door. Ah! she would, she was not so helpless, etc."

In terror, lest she should again bring on her fever, I yielded to every demand, and so peace came again.

In the long silence that followed, I noticed that the

wind was rising fast, that each blast was stronger and longer than the one preceding it, and that the old house trembled ominously under each fierce gust. The shadows, that earlier in the day had been content to linger in the corners, had with stealthy boldness advanced till they had filled the room with darkness, through which I heard the faint, fluttering breathing of the sick woman in her great bed, and the shrill scream of the wind as it swept across the lake to hurl itself upon the challenging city.

I rose at last to light the lamp, and lifting it, was about to place it back of the tall head-board of the bed, that its direct rays might not disturb the possible sleeper, when by chance the light fell full upon the painted face of the laughing, little Phil. The effect was wonderful; it seemed a face alive. The roguish eyes, the merry smile betraying the whitely even teeth, the little brown hand holding back the panting dog. He was joyous life personified, and I stood there wondering where the laughing child had found the courage to meet death so bravely; and, as if in answer to my thought, the faint voice of his mother came from the old bed, saying: "Yes, he was very brave, my man-child Philip, brave, brave! You know I saw it all. Aye, it was a good glass, a strong glass, and I saw. She was afraid, though she was the older, and her poor, blue eyes were strained and wild, and her quivering lips were white like her cheeks. But my Philip held her hand and stood still, while many raced madly to and fro. At one great, approaching wave I saw his lips move and I felt he cried, 'Mammy!' I, too, thought it was the end, but as it broke and surged away they were still standing hand in hand, and I knew Eternity in the moment I stood waiting there, waiting for that which came! There were cries and groans about me. The mighty wave seemed for one second to stand quite still, then with blinding, crushing force it struck its awful blow! It was enough; the solid deck sank swiftly from beneath their feet, the water rushed between their frightened, little lips into their laboring lungs, and it was over! With uplifted faces, and hands tight-clasped together, they went down before my tortured eyes! Ah, God! 'twas hard; in one hour my life made desolate! Yet will I worship Thee, forever! Hast Thou not said, 'the sea shall give up its dead'? Aye, and for that great promise I worship and bow down! By the word of the Lord were the heavens made. The word of the Lord is true!"

The thin, curiously faint voice sank into silence for a few moments. I placed the lamp as I had intended, and seated myself by her bedside again. She faced the lake—the curtains drawn entirely away from the window. I faced her, leaning slightly against the bed. Her eyes were nearly closed, but her lips were moving, and presently she said, as if continuing a conversation: "No, you do not care for her. No! because her golden head is high, and she holds the broken necklace in her hand. Why broken? Did he have second sight, that artist? Did he know, and was the broken necklace in her hand meant as a warning to me? You care for my man-child, because he laughs. You do not care for my 'gift-of-God,' because of an air, a manner; you are wrong. 'Tis but a way, a trick of movement. On my breast, with love-tightened, little arms about my neck, she was as sweetly lovable as the meekest little maiden in the land. And when they knelt in prayer, with folded hands, her head was bowed as humbly! Oh!" she suddenly cried, " Oh! not to have their sweet bodies to love and caress and care for, not to have their eager minds to guard, to direct, to develop!"

She moaned piteously, and then, giving a great sigh, she added: " But His word is true, and there is the sign to wait for "—and so sank into a long silence.

I was watching her closely, and suddenly she seemed to cease to breathe. I rubbed her hands; I called her loudly. She feebly opened her eyes and turned them toward the cupboard in the corner. I flew to it, and searching eagerly, I found two or three bottles there, one marked cordial. I administered some as quickly as I could, and saw her revive, but from that moment I was frightened, and I noted every word she spoke and every movement that she made. Her first words made me shiver. She said: " I am not afraid, girl Clara, but I must have the sign. I cannot go without it."

After a pause, while I resumed my seat facing her, she said: " It's very good of you to stay with me. Strange, after so many years alone, to have companionship at the last. Old Myra Worden watched over by an actress! Verily, the world does move!" A pause, and then she babbled on: "Ever since the night you came to me out of the storm and tried to be kind to me, I have known you were some way connected with the sign. You admired my treasures there, you loved my old laces, and sometimes I thought—I almost thought that you liked me."

"Dear Mrs. Worden," I cried, "I love you very much!" and I lifted the hand I was holding to my lips and kissed it. I felt her start, her black, old eyes flashed wide open, she gave me a piercing glance and exclaimed: "What?—what's that you say—you say —you——?"

I repeated with tears in my eyes: "I say, I love you very much," and again I pressed my lips upon her cold and trembling hand. She closed her eyes; she pressed her thin lips close, but could not hide their quivering, and presently, in almost a whisper, she murmured: "Fifty and odd years since those words were used to me. 'Tis almost like a foreign tongue. But, oh, my girl, my girl! it's mighty pleasant hearing. You—You—"

"I love you—I love you very much," I slowly and lowly repeated, and she nodded her head at each word, and, smiling faintly, sank into quietude. The time was long, the clock struck more than once, and she had not moved. My hand was holding hers. I feared to release it lest I might disturb her. The fire was long out, and I was cold. I wondered if she was asleep. I had twice been deceived on that subject, and dare not venture an opinion. I longed for dawn. Leaning on the bed, holding her hand closely in mine, I raised my tired eyes and began dully following the involved design carved upon the high head-board. I do not know just when I lost the design, but I felt no shock when I realized that I was looking at the lake, though I had not turned round. I wondered faintly how it could be, but I went on gazing quietly across the heaving, tossing, gray, repellant waste, and in the changes that followed I heard certain words, but whether those words were spoken by myself or fell from the lips of the ancient woman at my side, I shall never know. I only know I heard—I saw.

At first the sky was dull and gray and heavy, like the lake; but as I looked far, far off, where the sky and water met, there came a whiteness of the purity of snow, and it grew and spread and filled up all the sky so far as eye could reach, and then I heard a voice say, faint and low: "Can it be mist?"

And at the words the whiteness became lambent with living fire. As sheet-lightning plays across the summer sky, so this soft fire flashed on, in, through, up, down and across the milky wonder, while the lake—oh, marvelous! The heavy gray was gone, the water clear, pure, brilliant, vast—lay like a mighty crystal, and the voice murmured: "As a sea of glass!"

Presently this lambent whiteness began to throb and thrill with color; streams of pink and rose, of amber, blue or violet, played up and down the sky—a green so vivid, so acutely pure, that the voice, speaking from the great book, said: " A rainbow like unto an emerald."

Between me and that great background of living, opulent color I dimly saw a movement in the air, and then it thickened with crowding, opaque, white shapes, even as one has seen the air thicken with the white movement of the snow-flakes—so now, from horizon to zenith and to horizon again, all the air was filled with the swift-moving, never-resting, great, white-winged host, and ere the cry in my throat could escape my lips, these unnumbered ones fell apart into two vast bodies, while between them there lay straight across the bosom of the crystal waters a broad path of glittering light.

My heart was plunging wildly against my ribs when I heard the voice, so low, saying: " The sea knew Him—knew His voice—His touch! How the waves must have rushed upon the sand to kiss the precious foot-prints His sacred feet had made!" And while these words were uttered, out, far out, upon the glittering path arose a radiance, even then intense, almost beyond the power of mortal eye to bear; my swift lids fell to shield my dazzled sight. Yet one moment more I gazed and saw—I say I *saw* that supernatural radiance taking form and substance and assuming the attitude of most majestic humanity.

I could bear no more; I threw the sick woman's hand from me to clutch at my own strangling throat, and all was gone! I saw the carved head-board—nothing more!

Shaking like a leaf, I turned my head toward Mrs. Worden's face, and dimly I understood that, by some route of nerves, *her* vision had been conveyed to my brain. She sat there against her pillows gasping, her nostrils quivering, her black eyes fairly blazing. She passed her tongue across her parched lips, and I heard the low voice say: "It cannot be—no, it cannot! for He has said no man shall look upon His face! But it might be, perhaps, that! Oh! I can raise my eyes no higher—the light is blinding—and yet, and yet—oh! 'tis He! It is the Master!"

Her hands were clasped upon her breast, her body shaken by her laboring heart—while in terror of that recognition—her soft, white hair crisped itself, and moved upon her brow and hollow temples, while in a husky whisper she repeated: "'Tis *He!*—the All-Beautiful! Do I not see His sacred feet, beneath the falling robe press the gently yielding, watery path? Can He have come in fulfillment of the great promise?"

Then, with a piercing cry, she stretched out her arms pleadingly, saying: "Master! Master! I may not look upon the glory of Thy face, but Thou wilt hear me! Oh! Thou lover of little children—pause—pause! They lie so near Thee, but one step away! Thou wilt not pass them by! Summon them, Son of Mary! always pitiful to mothers, pity me! and summon them! Ah! the Hand is raised—the Blessed Hand, irradiating Light—is raised, and there—there—Oh King of Kings!—they are there! Hand clasped in hand—at the

Beloved Master's knee—they smile at me! they raise their little hands, and, Power Supreme! *they make the sign!*"

The room rang with her wild, triumphant cry of joy! She flung her frail arms wide, and repeated: "The sign! The sign!" then, "Yes, my dearies, mother's coming! We will fall down and worship, and then we will all go on together!"

Her arms dropped suddenly—her black eyes closed—and she fell sidewise into my arms; and even in the very moment of placing her upon her pillow I cast one glance through the uncovered window and saw but the sullen sky bending low over the still more sullen lake.

She never opened her eyes again, and as she lay there so still, so white, I could not but notice how gentle her face had grown, and bending down for the first and last time, I kissed her tenderly. A slow smile came about her lips, and she spoke for the last time, when she said softly, happily: "The sign! *It is* the sign!"

A moment later there was a long sigh, broken by a shiver, and then stillness, perfect stillness, and I whispered: "They have all gone on together!"

"In Paris Suddenly———"

"In Paris Suddenly ———"

I saw it in the *Herald* this morning: " In Paris suddenly, Madame de B———." Nothing remarkable about that announcement. Nothing to affect the general reader, but to me the letters were luminous.

"In Paris suddenly, Madame Miriam de B———." The creep is in my blood yet, for you see, I met Madame Miriam de B——— once, and if I were to live in this world even unto a hundred years, I should not forget that brief meeting.

The house was crowded; we were yet in the first act of the running play, one night, when a companion, a young society woman (who was trying to unlearn in a theatre all she had been taught as an amateur) edged close to me and whispered: " Look at the woman in the box; is she not beautiful ?"

I looked and answered quickly: " She is handsome, not beautiful."

" I can't see any difference between the meaning of the words," she pouted, " but look well at her, I have something to tell you when ———."

Here the action of the play parted us, but brought me close to the box. I had needed no urging to look well at its occupant. I could scarcely take my eyes from her, there was something so strange, so odd about her. She was not young. She was most stately in air and figure. Her head was most beautifully shaped, her features regular, her chin firm and deeply cleft, and her eyes—not black, not brown—yet dark, radiantly dark. Their soft shining seeming to contradict the cold strength of her face. Her brows—ah, at last, here was the bizarre touch! Her eyebrows formed one straight line. I don't mean that they nearly met or were thinly joined; they were thickly and darkly united, in one threatening sweep, above her glowing eyes, giving that hint of tragedy to her face that so surely accompanies united brows on either man or woman.

Once her eyes caught mine and calmly held them fast, and in that moment, as a child may flash a blinding ray of sunlight from a mirror into your face, there flashed into my mind these words: "Only a qualified admiration, eh? And you feel something, eh? You don't know what? No! and you won't know either, my dear!" and I ended the act with cheeks as hot from wounded feeling as though the words had actually been spoken to me.

I was not in the second act, neither was the "young society woman," or at least she was on the stage for about three minutes, after which she came, swelling visibly with importance, for in very truth she had something to reveal, and first exacting, on word of honor, promise not to tell (I only do it now, when: "In Paris suddenly———"). She quickly began: "You can see she is a lady, can't you? Born in Boston—perfectly lovely family—old—very old, you know! Was splendidly educated, and the very day of her *début* in society—I don't know who brought her out, her mother was dead, you know—that very day her father killed himself! Ruined—no courage and all that—she had no near relatives! Went off alone—went abroad—worked at teaching or companioning or something! Things then went wrong—troubles came, awful troubles! Oh—oh!" The speaker's eyes looked fairly scared, her hands trembled, she drew close to me, and holding fast a fold of my dress, she with desperate haste flung out these words: "She—that American woman—that lady sitting there—she has been accused of murder! Why, she has stood trial for her life!"

I could only gaze at her in stupid silence, and after a moment she rambled on about her uncle being Madame de B——'s lawyer, and his having charge of her affairs over here, as she would not live here—would not settle anywhere in fact—just wandered from place to place, etc.

At last I broke in, with a gasp: "Murderess! She a murderess? But why—how?"

"Oh!" cried my informant: "She was innocent, of course, or I should not know her (I had not thought of that). But she had a narrow escape, and owed it to a man she had always hated; to the dead man's valet."

Again, and more impatiently, I broke in: "But why—how—who?"

She caught the last word, "who," and went on: "Who was killed? Why, Count de Varney! He was a wicked, old wretch! Had a palsied arm, and was broken in health when Miriam first met him! Well, for years she bore his name, and she was the active mistress of his great, lonely home, and a most devoted nurse to him, but she was terribly alone! The servants, who disliked her because she was a foreigner, she ignored all save one, the Count's valet—him she loathed! She tried to have him sent away and failed, and he knew she had failed. Not a pleasant situation, was it? I must tell you, that in the left wing of the great building there was a room whose windows chanced to overlook those of the private apartments of the Count and Countess, in the main building. This peculiarity was well known, too, and highly valued by the spying servants, and from that room came the evidence that so nearly ruined their hated mistress. The Count had been improving, but as his strength increased his temper roughened, and one day, through one of his bursts of rage, she learned that she had been cruelly, deliberately betrayed—tricked!—by the merest mockery of a marriage; one that, in France at least, was utterly worthless! Surprise—anguish—shame—all at last were lost in fury! A fury so wild—so filled with threats—that the Count fairly quailed before it— begged to be spared a scandal—swore he would yet marry her—nay, he would now, this moment, draw up his will and make her his heiress! Give all to her in her maiden name—so that she should be protected, should aught happen to him before he could marry her! This will he proceeded to have drawn up at once, for you see, during those past years, Miriam had learned much of his outrageous past—knew more of his secret ill-doings than he quite realized—knew, indeed, that he had placed himself within the reach of law! And now, in her otherwise helpless anger, she determined to at least punish him with a great fright. So she secretly prepared and sent an unsigned letter, of seeming friendly warning, to the Count, telling him of the very worst of his past acts. That he had been discovered at last, and that by the evening of that day the officers would arrive at the *château* to arrest him! The letter came—Count de Varney read it! Miriam had thought to frighten him, and she succeeded so perfectly that the old man—white-lipped—rose from the table, and took his trembling way to his own room, where he hurriedly and clumsily hung himself."

"Why," I cried, "I thought you said he had been murdered?"

"Wait!" she said impatiently—"Wait! Over in the wing-room there was a woman, not spying on the movements of her master or mistress—she afterwards swore—but being in love with the valet, she was watching for him, and so happened to be a witness to the hanging of the old Count. No sooner—swore this woman—had her master kicked away the chair on which he had been standing, than a door opened and Madame de Varney entered. For one instant she stood apparently stunned by the sight before her—and then she laughed! She made no movement to call for help—she offered no help herself, but came closer to the writhing, horribly-struggling, hanging figure! The woman swore that once her master threw out his hand imploringly—that she thought he touched her mistress, she was so close to him—but she, the witness, turned faint just then at the awful drawing up of the hanging man's limbs and did not see quite clearly—but another servant joined just then, and both watched—and swore that only when the master was quite still did the mistress move, and then she went first to a desk and looked at some papers, and then rushed to the door, throwing it open and calling for help! She rang the bell violently, and the valet rushed in at her call, as if he had been standing at the very door—but before he made a movement to cut down the body, he spoke fiercely and rapidly to the Countess, and turned to the swaying figure of the Count de Varney, who had died horribly of slow strangulation!

"The trial was long, for that part of the world. The scandal was great, the mock-marriage being scoffed at and Madame Miriam de B—— treated simply as an adventuress. The will in her favor told against her greatly, but, to the stupefaction of every one, the valet defended her—swearing *he* had seen his master before his mistress had—that he was *dead before she entered the room*—that he had gone for help, not wishing to touch the body without a witness being present, etc. She swore that her husband was dead when she found him—but without the valet she would certainly have been condemned to long, long imprisonment at the very least. She lives under an assumed name now, and just wanders over the world, as houseless as ———"

"Third act; everybody ready!" shouted the call-boy.

I looked about in a bewildered way for my fan and my handkerchief, and went to my place on the stage, saying to myself: "I will not look that way again to-night."

The third act was known, in theatrical parlance, as the strong act of the play. In it I had to attempt to poison my rival, who had formerly been my beloved friend, and at the very last moment, when the poison was at her very lips, with a strong revulsion of feeling, I had to snatch it away and swallow it myself, and then proceed with the death scene, which naturally followed.

I had kept my promise; I had not looked once toward the stage box. I had worked myself well into my character again and was doing my best to be *it*, and not myself. That night I had just reached my half unconscious victim and was cautiously raising the poisoned drink to her lips, when some absolutely *outside* power dragged my unwilling eyes from her face and left me staring straight into the eyes of the woman "who had been tried for her life"!

The actress beside me wondered what had happened —what I had forgotten! No fly enmeshed in spider's web was ever held more helplessly than I was held for a moment's time by that devilish face, leaning from the shadow of the curtained box. Strained and eager, it was white as chalk. The lips were parted—the nostrils quivering—while her thunderous brows frowned fiercely above the cruel eyes that held me! And while I looked, so surely as ever Murder raised its head to look through human eyes, so surely Murder triumphant looked at me through hers!

The actress at my side made a faint movement; the spell was broken! I gave the shuddering cry that belonged to the situation, and raising the glass to my own lips, quickly swallowed the poison, and at the very moment of so doing, from the private box, low, but perfectly distinct, came the contemptuous words: "You fool! You fool!"

I went on with my scene and ended the play.

At the end no sign of approbation came from the private box. With some irritation, I asked myself if she expected me to change the action of a play to gratify her savage taste?

The box was what is called a "stage-box," and it is generally held by the manager for his family, or for visiting artists, as it is apt to open just inside the stage door. As I approached, I saw the box door open. Two or three steps led up to it. At the foot of them stood the young lady who had told me the story, and who was the hostess of Madame de B——. She saw me and called: "Madame wishes to see you!"

Madame de B—— looked her name—Miriam—as she stood there. Her stately figure was so beautiful, her face so calm and handsome—but I shrank from her now; I could not forget the face I had seen but a few moments ago. She stood at the top of the steps; I was one step lower, while her young hostess waited at the door. She did not speak. I noted the elegance of her gown, and followed the movement of her white, ungloved hands as she raised some black lace to drape about her head and shoulders—Spanish fashion—and so I met her eyes, and instantly there was neither theatre nor hostess—there was nothing—there was no one, but just she and I. I set my teeth hard and bore her look. A hot flush swept over me, then I felt my eyebrows lifting of their own accord, a faint chill crept slowly about the roots of my hair, and presently I saw the evil, hot light glowing in her eyes again, and dreading the coming of what I had seen there before, I spoke suddenly, imploringly, and said: "O Madame, *was* he dead, or *was* he alive, when you found him?"

Her lips drew back in silent laughter, her eyes danced in burning triumph: "*Alive! Alive!! Poor, little fool! Alive!!*" and then she leaned over me, and gripping me hard upon the shoulders, she looked deep down into my eyes, and then she said slowly, with the devil in her face: "I—wonder—what—became—of—that—devoted—valet?"

She laughed aloud, turned suddenly to gather up her skirt, and I threw out my hand and felt my way by the wall, down the steps, and so into my own dressing room, where I burst into wild sobbing.

Two or three nights passed, and then my friend remarked that dear, handsome Madame de B—— had sailed again.

"It was funny, she said, "the idea of asking you to come to her box, and then never opening her lips to you, wasn't it?"

I looked stupidly at her: "Why, what do you mean?" I asked. "You stood in the door all the time—you must have heard her speaking?"

"Why, she never opened her lips—except when she laughed, as you went out!"

I was sorely puzzled—until perhaps a week after—*apropos* of nothing, my little chatter-box remarked: "You know poor Madame de B——.was one of Count de Varney's nurses at the very first of their acquaintance. He was a victim of insomnia. A doctor called the Count's attention to her. She used to make him sleep, sometimes even against his will. The doctor said she had most unusual *mesmeric* power."

We never spoke again of Madame de B——, but sometimes on an autumn night, dark and chill, with the rain falling stealthily on the sodden leaves that give forth no rustle when a cautious foot presses them, I have caught myself repeating those ominous words: "I—wonder—what—became—of—that—devoted—valet?" But now to that query there can be but one answer: "In Paris suddenly, Madame de B——."

Two Buds.

Two Buds

"There is no poetry in life to-day!" We were walking down Euclid Avenue, and my friend had been expressing her hot disapproval of many things in this really excellent world of ours, ending with that youthfully positive assertion: "There is no poetry in life to-day!"

I mildly suggested that she might not recognize it as poetry, if she saw it, as poems were not always bound in white and silver nor yet in blue and gold—some, indeed, never reaching the honor (?) of binding at all.

By the fierceness of her contempt for the opinion of another, one could easily measure her utter inexperience, but she finally closed her address by haughtily informing me that she was not to be deceived by "bindings"—that all poetry was sacred to her, whether she found it in the polished, metrical form of verse, or simply expressing itself in human action—but in these days there was no poetry—conscious or unconscious—for—she got no further; my fingers were on her wrist in that unintentionally savage clutch that never fails to secure immediate attention and later remembrance—and I was whispering: "Look! Look well! at the old man approaching!"

I'm sure, though, she needed no such reminder—no one could help looking at him—and, at first glance, only his snowy hair kept the laugh from one's lips. A well-grown boy of twelve would have been "mad as a hopper" if he had not stood, at least, even in height with this old, old man. His gait was half-trot, half-shuffling walk, and his speed remarkable—but little as he was, he leant forward in a peculiar way. His nationality, after fifty-five unbroken years in America, was stamped so clearly on face and figure that his tongue's thick, disobedient English was not needed to proclaim him an ancient Dutchman. His garments would have wrung laughter from a telegraph pole—the saddest thing on earth. That his wife made his trousers there could be no doubt, for if you looked at *them* only, you could never tell which way the man was going to walk. Then, short as his little legs were, his trouser-legs were still shorter, while he could have stowed away quite a nice, little outfit in that portion of them known as the "slack." This breadth of beam and shortness of keel gave to the public gaze a generous margin of clean, white stocking. His collar, which was an integral part of his shirt—and not, to use his own words, "a flimsy-flamsy yump-a-bout-ting what wont stay hitched!"—was of immaculate whiteness, but utterly innocent of starch, and on his venerable head he wore an antique, "panama" hat. A Dutch friend, who cultivated coffee, had picked this "panama" in Java, when it was green—so to speak—and sent it here, and the older citizens had, for twenty-odd years, watched its slow ripening under the American sun—and in its wearer's eyes it had just reached its prime. Before the quaint, little body reached us, I whispered: "It is not poverty that makes him dress like that—he owns the big 'Buckeye Block,' besides his dwelling-house up town, and I saw her eye renew its slackening hold on him, so great is our unconscious deference to money that already he seemed less grotesque to her, because she saw him through the softening, yellow light his gold cast upon him—and then he dragged off his well-ripened "panama," and stopped to tell me " youst how glad vas he to see me!"

For he had entered this country j-less, and j-less he remained, using y in place of j with such smiling confidence that it was "all right" that no one had the heart to sternly put him in the wrong by correcting him. My wise, young friend smiled quite brightly upon him, and when he had passed, demanded of me all I knew about him, "because he was such a dear—and so individual—you know!"

I assured her there was nothing to tell—that he was simply an ignorant but honest man, who by the hardest work and almost incredible economy had risen to wealth, and she surprised me by replying "that there was more than that in his face, even for her, a stranger, to see—and what was the secret of the almost child-like gentleness of his clear, blue eyes?"

Whereupon, we lunched in a quiet corner of a quiet room and over many—too many—cups of coffee, I told her that his name was Knights—Jacobus Knights—and I had made his acquaintance while I was still so young that the salient features of my own personality were the length of my braids and the whiteness of my aprons. He used to rear vegetables and then sell them from a cart, which he pushed when it was full and dragged when it was empty. Being sent after him one day by a lady, I called out lustily: "Boy—boy—you boy! Stop—stop—I say!" thus making the mistake that many an older and wiser person made daily, and one that was greatly facilitated by the tailless jacket and flat cap the little man wore. Really, it savored of the uncanny to thus address a question to the back of childhood and receive your answer from the unshaven lip of maturity. He seemed to be quite used to the error, and only laughed and said: "Dat is noddings—youst noddings at all! Whad I make mit you—onion—squash—eh, whad now?"

Two years later I came to live on S—— street, and right opposite, little Mr. Knights had his little playhouse of a home, his doll of a blond baby, and his tremendous wife. No, her size was not the result of comparison, she was really a tremendously big woman, from whose deep chest and strong, column-like throat there issued the thin, little voice of a complaining, "cheeping" chick too weak to break its imprisoning shell. She was a spring of pure Dutch undefiled. Not one English sentence could she command, but she was a friendly creature, and hobnobbed deprecatingly but successfully with her neighbors through the medium of a ponderous but expressive and ever-smiling pantomime.

Never were such workers known before. I doubt if they could have recognized their own breakfast had they met it, by daylight. Certainly they had, for at least forty years, taken that meal by artificial light—candle or oil, whichever was the cheaper. Any morning between half-past four and five o'clock the neighbors could see, through the dim light, a pretty little incident. The cart, heavily laden, stood outside the gate; the small pedler with the boy-body and the man-face, with a broad, leather band or collar across his neck, hooked its ends to the shafts of the cart, thus placing on his shoulders part of the heavy weight and at the same time causing the curious forward bend of body that disfigured his walk to-day. When he was quite ready for his start, the door opened and the big woman appeared, holding in her brown arms a little, night-gowned figure, its bare, pink feet curled up in her one broad hand—baby dreams still lingering mistily in the sleepy, blue eyes, and while one wee hand pushed back impatiently the blond tangle of curls, the other one tossed uncounted kisses to the father dimly seen, while a sweet, bird-like voice cried: "Bye-bye, Papa! Bye-bye! Ick lief dy! Bye-bye!"

For this little one had the gift of tongues, and from babyhood Dutch and English were simply convertible terms with her—and the adoring father, with cap off, stood and smiled, and smiled, and waved his earth-stained, stumpy hand, and blessed her with all the tender Dutch blessings that he knew, and then put on his cap—took up his load and started on the way that would have been so hard, so ugly, but for those baby kisses that bloomed like flowers on his path and sweetened all his day. When he had gone quite out of sight the little Rosie was returned to the great, Dutch bed to complete her sleep, and in a few moments the mother was crouching between the rows of vegetables, looking like a monster toad, and was weeding—weeding—weeding, until with almost breaking back she began to carry water and sprinkle—sprinkle—sprinkle, and after that the household tasks of other women began—washing—scrubbing —ironing—baking, yet always and ever with it all, there were little, white garments for Rosie, and time to put them on, and when the child outgrew the vegetable basket she had passed a great part of her life in, playing with a few marigolds or a hollyhock flower—she could not have salable ones like mignonette or pinks —the mother feared many things—for, as "Little Knights" (that was what the neighbors called him), explained in slow, back-end-first sentences, the vegetable basket arrangement had been very satisfactory to both parties, and his wife could plant or hoe or weed without anxiety, having simply to put out her hand now and then and pull the basket after her. But now that was all past, and his wife was "full up mit dem fears," and when questioned as to the nature of the fears that were filling her up, his blue eyes seemed both surprised and reproachful that they could not see for themselves the possible dangers in small Rosie's path. "In place of first," he explained, "der was de cleanness—she mighd get dirty de garden in! Den," his eyes grew round at that, "der vas de red-peppers—she might touch dem and aftervards rup her sveet eyes!" but when at the end of a long list of possibilities, he cried out: "Unt dem pees—dem honey pees—what pite mit dere tails—suppose dey make mit dere stingers on her? Ach Gott! Ach Gott!" and, caught in a linguistic tangle, he fell into deep Dutch, from which he emerged breathless and excited. Now that is a condition no Dutchman will endure, so without apology, he trotted off home to soothe himself with the one smoke he allowed himself each day, and then to—rest? Oh, no, there was much work done in that small house by night as well as by day—and mind, there are old neighbors still to support this statement — they used actually to work in the garden by moonlight — not habitually, but often enough, Heaven knows! And what was the object of all this ceaseless labor—of their astonishing economies?

Before the coming of their baby girl, they had been little more than two patient, dumb beasts of burden. Born and bred to work—they worked—but dully—without hope or special object—but when God had sent into their lives that laughing, pretty thing, and formed her delicately that she might arouse their tenderness, they had changed. They looked at one another, and each, smiling, saw the other anew. They dreamed for her—they hoped now for her—they prayed now heavy, laborious, loving prayers for her. Truly she had been the "locust and wild honey" that fed them in their wilderness—so now it was for her they labored and were therefore never tired.

As the years passed I, who had long since ceased to live in S—— street, often went there to visit my friends who had remained, stopping with them from Saturday till Monday, and these visits kept me still in touch with "Little Knights" and his idol. It seemed strange that Rosie was quite unspoiled by so much adulation. She was a favorite with all the neighbors, was polite and obedient outside her own domain, while within it, an absolute monarch, she ruled with gentlest strength her idolatrous subjects. Derision or contempt shown to them was swiftly and sharply resented by her, while the only time she had to sternly exert her authority was when she made some demand upon the treasury that was for *their* benefit instead of hers.

The Knights' Sunday went like this: When it was time for Sunday-school the front door opened (mind you, in any other family of like position in life, that door would have opened for only one of three things— a wedding, a funeral, or the first visit of the clergyman, so think how they honored that mere child)—then big Mrs. Knights appeared and brushed the step over with a cloth and retired from view (a pause), then little Rosie appeared, balancing a moment on the step like one of her own pet, white doves, her many short skirts and her white dress starched to the uttermost limit of rattling stiffness, open-work white stockings and black slippers, with an ankle strap fastened with a gold button, a broad, pink sash about her waist, pink ribbon bows on each long, blond braid, a big leghorn hat secured first by an elastic band, and over that by broad, pink ribbons tied in a large bow under her milk-white chin. In her little, mitted hands she held a testament, and from between its leaves peeped a pink or a rose— a handkerchief the size of a large postage stamp finished her outfit—and so, gravely and with great propriety, she came down the narrow path between the "flox" and "sweet-william," the "larkspur" and "four o'clocks," and all the horde of strong-growing, free-blooming flowers of the poor—herself the daintiest flower of them all—and at the gate she turned and kissed her hand to the two heads thrust out at either side of the door—the fresh-shaven face of her father low down on one side, the broad-smiling face of her mother high up on the other—then walked sedately on towards the church, while behind her, the heads gone, the door closed, seemingly of its own volition—to open no more until the next week.

A few minutes later Mrs. Knights appeared at the side door where there was a tiny, *tiny* little platform, with "scarlet-beans" trained thickly over its morsel of roof. On this porch one chair was carefully placed on Sunday mornings and occupied by Mrs. Knights, arrayed in a white petticoat and white bedgown (as the short, loose garment was called). Her hair was oiled and brushed to a glassy smoothness, a big horn-comb loomed high above her head, and a pair of gold ear-drops, that seemed to have been sold by the yard, dangled from her ears. Her tired, old feet rested in a hugh pair of braided list shoes that looked liked boats. Once seated, "Little Knights" trotted out with a Bible of a size so prodigious one wondered how it ever found a resting place inside that little bit of a house. Its mighty clasps undone, he placed it on his wife's lap, and then made another trip and brought out a great pair of spectacles, framed in silver, which he solemnly fitted on her nose, then most carefully and cautiously he adapted himself to such narrow margin of floor space as was left for him, and their service began.

It was with a rather wavering, quavering rendering of an old hymn, after which Mrs. Knights opened the book, and looking over the tops of her glasses—she could not see a word through them, but she felt they loaned her a certain dignity as of office—she found the place, and by the aid of one blunt finger (its stained, cracked nail worn down to the very quick), she made her way with pathetic slowness across the page of frenzied Dutch print. Not that they doubted the saving-power of the English Bible for the English and incidentially for the American sinner, but they felt that their own sins were so peculiarly Dutch in quality that nothing short of a Dutch Bible could save them. Wherefore, Mrs. Knights, each Sunday, with blunt fore-finger seemed to dig out words of Holy-writ from the great book, while her small husband carefully stored them in the basket of his memory.

After the chapter had come to its laborious close, they both took breath and wiped their dripping brows, then clasped their hands, bowed their heads and offered each a silent prayer. I had once come upon them so, the bees circling about their gray, old heads, while their prayers, like the perfume of two souls mingling with the perfume of the flowers, rose through the warm air, straight to that great God who had given them Rosie.

And that sweet name encompassed all of good his life contained—health and strength, growing wealth and the respect in which his neighbors held him, and when he would have offered humble thanks for them, instead he blessed God for Rosie.

With a slight trace of that peasant cunning which had been his when the stocking-foot had been his only bank, he tried to hide, as far as possible, his increasing prosperity. He had long owned the double lot and the toy house that made home for him, and it was whispered that certain lots on the outskirts of the town, used by "Little Knights" for a truck-garden, were really his, though the wily Jacobus often, perhaps too often, referred to the fact: "Dat he had paid de rent dem gartens of!" However, the old neighbors to this day tell a story of "Little Knights" touching upon his secretiveness about money.

Rosie, who, by the way was Rosie to all the world

except her father—he called her ever and always his Rose or his "Little Rose;" in babyhood, or in womanhood, "My Rose" was the name he gave his idol! When his Rose had reached the age of fourteen, she stood before him one evening, holding a match to his pipe, and when the tobacco glowed evenly all over, she shut down the perforated silver cover, and said suddenly: "Father, I wonder if you can be rich enough to buy me something, an expensive something, too, father?" and the old eyes had fairly danced, and surely in that moment, Jacobus Knights tasted all the sweetness of prosperity. Yet, Jacobus was a Dutchman, and therefore cautious, and so assuming as much doubt as was possible over so absolutely certain a matter, he inquired as to the nature of "dis ting vat made such expense mit itself," and Rosie, with clear eyes on his face, had answered with a little tremble of anxiety in her voice: "A piano, father."

And the small father had crushed back a smile, and averted joyous eyes, and had basely suggested that an accordeon "might answer youst as well."

But clever Rosie noticed he said no word about not affording it, so she instantly assumed a patient look of endurance, saying: "No father, an accordeon will not do; but never mind, I see you are not rich enough yet, I can wait!" and he had hastily broken in on this meekness with: "*You see, you see,* youst noddings, my Rose! How many dimes a hunnert tollars, makes dem bianos mit demselves, all mit der india-rupper overcoats on 'em, too, unt lots of dat moosic pieces sphilt all de top over? All—youst all de nice hair-horse biano stools, too, vat twist round unt round, and make you sick mit yourself—everyting vat goes dat biano mit? *Dat* is, vat I come rich enough to give mit my Rose!"

But imagine the stupefaction of every soul who knew "Little Knights," when two weeks later, without a word of his intentions to anyone, he sent men to lay the foundation of a new house on the next-door lot, which was vacant; and to the excited inquiries of his neighbors he *naively* replied, between puffs of smoke: "Vell, you see now, my Rose, she vant dat biano, unt—(pause)—unt I have to make first de house to put him in—don't you see mit me?" And the laugh that followed rolled around the town and made him known far and wide as the little, Dutch gardener who built a house for his daughter's piano.

A few more prosperous years and "Little Knights," who began to be called "Little Old Knights" now, was watching, with proud eyes, the growing train of Rosie's lovers. She was a charming girl—clever, well-read, an excellent musician, a perfect little housekeeper, and, best of all, tenderly, bravely loyal to her big, illiterate mother and her short-cut, old father.

She was a milk-white blond—a silvery, flaxen blond, and though tints of mauve and clear, pure blue found favor in her eyes, she still wore pink for her old father's sake. He had used to say of her in baby days: "My

Rose is such a vite, liddle Rose—I like dat she be tied up pink ribbons mit—alvays mit pink!" So now, tied up "mit pink," she received her young friends in that one-time "holy of holies"—the front room; now termed parlor. With a sort of anguished pride big Mrs. Knights saw sunlight streaming through only thin lace curtains across the new carpet—saw other books than the Bible and family album there—saw flowers and open piano, and oh—oh—the chairs all pulled out from their nice, straight rows against the wall! But then—ach Gott! Rosie knew! And the ringing of the door-bell was as music in the ears of the doting, old pair who sat in the inner room—one knitting, the other smoking—both nodding and smiling and putting severe restraint upon themselves to keep from rushing in with refreshments before greetings were hardly over.

That moment of offering refreshments was a moment of joy and of torture. They would willingly have effaced themselves from the life of their "American" daughter (as they proudly called her), but she had neither friend nor acquaintance who did not know—and through her introduction—her father and mother. With regard to the latter, Rosie had worked a miracle. In two years' time, by faithful and almost desperate effort, she had taught her mother nine simple English words. They were evidently selected by the astute Rosie with a view to future social requirements. So now Mrs. Knights could, with portentous gasps and moistening brow, say: "How do-do?" "Com' again!" "Good-bye!" "Ver' glad!" "Ver' sorry!" and "My!" And when the moment came for the long-necked bottles of sparkling German wine—the fruit—the sandwiches—the cream-cheese, etc., to appear, the old pair, rejoicing in their hospitality, swelling with pride in Rosie and Rosie's popularity, yet nearly crushed by embarrassment, appeared, too. And Mrs. Knights—"How do-do?" all round—wilted into a big chair in the corner, from whence she smiled most happily and cast a "My!" of excellent pronunciation into the general conversation now and then, for which her Rosie gave her a dozen kisses afterward.

The bright, laughing girl saw that her father had the prettiest visitor in the room to sit by, and that her own choice of the young men should wait upon her mother, and so, with wonderful tact, she led them into her brighter life, instead of shutting them out into the shamed solitude known to so many lowly parents. Rosie was nineteen when she made her choice. Young Randall had been a child of wealth until, at twenty, his father tried to "corner" something and had been cornered himself and ruined. Then the boy went to work and had been working for six years when he fell in love with Rosie. Never had there been such excitement in a Dutchman's life before! Little Old Knights was a house-building, present-buying, hand-rubbing, amiable, little lunatic! His wife smiled in her very sleep at night, and lived in her Dutch receipt-book all day, while Rosie had to watch the pair with the eyes of an affectionate lynx to prevent them from buying horsehair furniture for her future parlor, and large chunks of amethyst or big, diamond-set things for ornaments.

But she managed so well that only a few atrocities crept in among her gifts, and her little home was charming. Many thought that now, as Rosie entertained a good deal and had new friends in her new home, she would ignore the old folks. Not she! Whenever she had anything "on," from a "coffee-drinking" to an "evening party," she flew down to the old home and laced her mother into shape, crowding her into a stiff, silk gown, that creaked at each labored breath of its wearer, and when she was in full panoply of war, and Little Old Knights had been turned about and looked over as if he were a boy getting ready for Sunday-school, Rosie kissed them both and took them off to her own home, and set them down in two big chairs with a little table between them, for their spectacles and handkerchiefs and other small belongings—and there, like an old pair of children, they sat and enjoyed all that went on; and when there was dancing, "Old Knights" never failed to indulge in one waltz with his ancient wife— the memory of whose youth must have gone into her feet to make her so light on them still. And while Rosie joined in the laughter this waltz always aroused, there would be a tremor in her voice and she would hold her young husband's hand close and whisper: "Will you love *me* like that, Hal, when I have grown old?"

So on radiant wings time flew by, until one morning neighbors heard laughing in "Little Knights'" garden —laughing that continued and continued, and when they went over, "Little Knights" was doing the laughing, with tears running down his cheeks and falling on the prodigious Bible open on his short knees. When questioned, he exclaimed: "She has kom'—all safe, she has kom'! I seen her mit mine eyes—I have tooched her mit dese fingers! De liddle daughter of mine own Rose! Ach, de Almighty Gott is a most goot Gott!" and then he bowed his white head and muttered: "Now let Thy servant depart mit peace!" And so poor, "Little Old Knights" found his cup of joy full to the brim!

And what happens to any cup held in human hands if filled to the brim? It runs over—and there is cruel loss! And so it came to pass that Rosie's little one stayed with them just long enough to smile a recognition of her girlish mother's face, and then some sweet, strong call came from the "beyond" that baby had heard and answered—and they were left to wonder at the awful void that small absence made in all their lives.

Poor, Old Knights! Tight in his arms he held the tiny, coffined dead—moaning over and over: "My liddle pud—my Rose's liddle pud!"—until that sad moment when, by sheer force, they took the wee, dead thing from him, to hide it away beneath the flowers and the grasses.

Time passed slowly now. Rosie, very gentle—very tender of others—was sad, so sad. That was not natural to her—so all rejoiced when hope once more shone in her face—and all was thankful when Little Old Knights trotted from door to door with the news that his Rose had "anodder liddle daughter—so like—ach Gott! so like de first—as never yet dey saw!"

Rosie's joy was great, but it was not the laughing, unthinking joy of other days. She felt anxieties and fears. She dreaded this and that, but her silvery blond baby was so strong and well, and grew so fast, and "crowed" and laughed, and romped with father and grandfather, and stood so strong upon her little legs that fears had to give way to confidence, and her heart bounded with triumph when she heard the baby voice, cry imperatively; "Ma—ma! ma—ma!"

One day in particular Rosie always remembered—she had toiled for a good hour at training baby to say: "Pa—pa," when the father had come from the office—and when he came the baby had stretched out her arms to him, looked back roguishly at Rosie, and then fairly screamed: "Ma—ma! ma—ma!" and they had all laughed and laughed! Good God! how easy it is for a baby to fill a happy home with merriment! And that very night "croup" had clutched with murderous fingers the little throat that was used to swell with laughter as a bird's throat swells with song—and darkness and silence came upon the house.

Little Knights—poor, broken, Little Knights—like a

small, gray shadow, flitted back and forth between the two stricken homes. At one moment he had blasphemed in his misery. His Rose had been lying on his breast and she had wrung her hands and lifted her tortured eyes to his and cried: "Father, what have I done? Think back—think hard! What wickedness did I do, that God should punish me so cruelly? Did I lie? Did I bear false witness against any one? Think father—think for me, dear!"

And then he had lifted up his voice against Almighty God and cursed his work—and now he remembered his words and shivered, for, with creeping horror, he felt that there was something approaching him more terrible even than the loss of the second little bud of love and hope—Rose! Rose—his worshiped Rose—who wept not —who thought no more for others' comforts —who sat motionless for long hours at a time, had been taken possession of by a grotesquely horrible idea that the husband she loved so was trying to put her legally away, because her children died! And she would hold his hands and beg piteously that he should wait for her to die!—that she would not be long about it now! And the poor husband would kneel at her feet and pour out his love and grief, but all in vain!

Then she would lay her head on "Little Knights'" breast and tell him to take her away before the new wife came! He felt what was coming, and believed *his* blasphemy had brought destruction upon her when his Rose became quite mad! At first he tried to take his life, but Mrs. Knights seemed to have eyes all over—he could not escape them. Then, suddenly, he cast himself—helpless, hopeless, almost heartbroken, at the "Blessed Feet," asking nothing for himself, but entreating mercy for his Rose!—so innocent, so good! Bye and bye he ceased to bargain with the Lord, and bowed his head, and with grief-shaken voice, said simply: "Thy will, not mine, O Gott!" and straight a gleam of sunlight came back into his life. Rose—his beloved Rose—had recovered her reason! "Little Knights" held her in his arms and kissed the weary eyes and drooping lips—and blessed God for her! but knew in his heart he would never again see his white Rose "tied up mit pink ribbons."

And time goes on and on, and Rose, gentle, kind, a very angel of mercy to the poor, devoted to her husband and her parents—rarely smiling—never laughing—shivers at the sight of a blond baby. Four years had passed after her second loss, and her silence was deceiving them all. I think, when one Sunday in church a strange, little, restless creature in her pew crept along the seat and put its baby hand on hers, and poor Rosie at that touch had fainted dead away, after that they understood.

One day I saw "Little Knights" standing uncovered at the side of two tiny graves. A small white stone at their head had carved upon it two rose-buds and beneath, three words, clear and plain: "Our little buds!" I murmured the words half aloud, and "Little

Knights," with tears on his cheeks, said: "**Yays, yays**—youst liddle puds—but, oh, whad sweet, liddle puds dey were! Gott give me youst von Rose—full bloomed unt perfect—but dese puds? *No! no!* He say dey may not bloom here!"

He looked up into the clear, far, far blue, and smiled and nodded, and said, very low: "Oop dere—I think He make 'em bloom out full—dem puds! I like I can see dat! I don't want to leaf my Rose—I stay here as long as she stay—but I vant so much to see my liddle puds bloom!" and then he placed on each wee grave a beautiful rosebud, and trotted away home to his good, old wife and his adored Rosie!

"Let me see," I added, "this is Saturday—is it not? Well, to-morrow, before four o'clock in the afternoon, should you go to W—— Cemetery, you would see the 'little hop o' my thumb' I pointed out to you a while ago come trotting in, holding two beautiful, exquisitely beautiful, rosebuds in his hand; would see him make his way to those two tiny graves, and without shame, fall on his knees, and with one arm stretched across the graves, humbly pray. Then kissing both buds, he would place one on each grave—then, with falling tears, leave the cemetery—and that has been done and will be done, winter as well as summer, by this poor, faithful 'Little Old Knights.'"

I glanced at my companion and was amazed to see her eyes were brimming, and as she dashed the tears away, the shameless little turncoat cried—"And do you now tell me you can't see poetry in life—when you have known a man like that? Why, there is all the poetry of 'fatherhood' right before your eyes!"

And to this day she wonders why I laughed so long and heartily.

The Ambition of MacIlhenny

The Ambition of MacIlhenny

After mentioning that last name it seems like rank waste of time to say his first name was Sandy. He couldn't help it, his parents couldn't help it, no one could help it; one name follows the other naturally.

Well, then, being Sandy MacIlhenny, of course he was Scotch. I mention it for mere form's sake, as you knew it beforehand, just as you knew what his first name was. But, fortunately for us all, he had lived in America so many years that he had lost or thrown away his dialect, and the only thing in his speech that could suggest his native heath was the marked preference for the letter "u" instead of "i" in whisky, (and I think, myself, "whusky" has a more filling sound) and a "burring," a b'r'r'r to his "r's," as though a very large, bewildered "bumble-bee" were blundering about the end of his broad tongue, and then bumping back to the roof of his mouth.

Poor MacIlhenny's life was a tragedy, and yet it was played, to the very last act, to an accompaniment of jeers and laughter—not malicious, not bitter, but simple, thoughtless laughter.

A description of his personal appearance might, I think, go a good way toward explaining the cause of that general laughter. Had he been simply ugly, all had been well—there's nothing injurious in ugliness; it may even be a power. He was worse than that. In our English language there is a word that may have been created at the very moment of Sandy's birth, for the express use of those wishing to describe him perfectly but briefly—that word is "grotesque."

He was tall, very tall, with a sudden, rounding droop of the shoulders that gave him the look of a buttonhook or interrogation point, while his thickness through the body was about that of a choice, salt codfish. If he was furnished with the usual number of internal organs they must have been pressed like autumn leaves in a dictionary, or else he did not wear them all at one time; that's how thin he was. Then he was the only tall man I ever saw pacing through life on bowed-legs. No, not knock-kneed! Sandy's legs were bowed to a roundness that let one see, at a glance, just how a picture of certain portions of the landscape would look in a perfectly round frame. No man on earth could command respect while standing on a pair of legs like Sandy's, unless they were concealed beneath the protecting petticoat of church or college. He had very high cheek-bones, across which the skin was drawn so tightly that they looked like a pair of unexpected knuckles. His chin was long and straight, without the slightest indentation or curve about it. His nose shared in the general lengthiness and was thin and pointed, while, owing to the narrowness of his entire structural plan, each small, greenish-blue eye turned inwardly and gazed with fixed resentment at the intervening bridge that seemed to be crowding them.

And these cruelly crossed eyes made MacIlhenny a veritable joy to the street boys, who would follow him, performing warlike dances, and then rush before him and wait at street corners with ostentatiously crossed forefingers between which they gravely spat to avert the ill-luck his glance might put upon them.

Poor man! In no limb, no feature had he been spared —so that the final touch of common, coarse ugliness was found in the shining baldness of the top of his head, and the little flounce of brick-red hair with which he seemed to be modestly trying to cover its startling nudity.

With such a body to dwell in, one can hardly wonder that his mind should become distorted and develop only in one direction, as it were, and such a direction, for the ambition of MacIlhenny, this poor, cross-eyed, bowlegged Scotchman of the lower laboring class— this excellent cutter of stone, was to be the greatest *tragic-actor* of his day!

Nor was his ambition of the mere "I wish I were!" or "I would like to be!" order. It was a devouring passion.

A strong word, "devouring," but since Webster says it means, among other things, "to consume ravenously, to prey upon, to swallow up, to appropriate greedily," it is the right word, for his mad ambition, even in its beginning, appropriated greedily all his small savings, all his spare time. It consumed his sense of duty toward his wife—he had no sense of the ridiculous to consume. It preyed upon his heart as well as his mind, and finally it swallowed up his very life.

Many of the old acting plays he knew by heart, had memorized literally from cover to cover, while his knowledge of Shakespeare's unacted plays was greater than most actors' knowledge of the acting ones. Quite naturally he was given over to the habit of quoting, in season and out of season, and it was an indulgence in this habit that brought the stonecutter into touch with the actors of the city.

There was a saloon not far from the theatre, and MacIlhenny, being at work near by, went in one noon for his mid-day beer. There was a party of actors there eagerly discussing the morning news of the death of one of their profession, a very well known and successful actor. Now, as they all knew, one of this party had been the envious enemy of the dead man, and now, instead of a respectful silence, they were astonished to see him assuming deep grief. There was a great pulling of moustaches and exchanging of glances, but no one replied, and the hypocrite burst out again, first with fulsome praise, and then with exaggerated expressions of sorrow. The last word was barely spoken, when a voice with a burr in it gravely and most distinctly remarked: "The tears live in an onion that should water this sorrow!"

There was an instant of surprised silence, in which every one recognized the exquisite fitness of the quotation, and then a roar of laughter — another and another! Many beers were thrust upon the Scotch stonecutter, who knew his Shakespeare so well—and —and—oh! poor MacIlhenny! Straightway he neglected his work; he loitered too long at his nooning. He could not tear himself away from the actors, who listened to his quotations and laughed at his antics, as children might laugh at the capers of a monkey. But MacIlhenny left them with a wild gleam in his poor, crossed eyes, with jumping, twitching muscles about his thin lips, fairly drunk with excitement.

It was on one of these occasions that he saw his landlord ahead of him in the public street—a rotund, little person who seemed to have had one story left off when he was built. He knew it, too, and tried, with piled up dignity and high silk hat, to make up the missing height. And it was to this dignified, black-croated, slow-moving, old gentleman that MacIlhenny roared: "Turn, hell-hound, turn! Turn, I say! I want to hand you me month's rent and save a trip to your house to-morrow!"

That was one of his out of season quotations, for the dignified old party was no hell-hound, but MacIlhenny had just been discussing Macbeth, and showing how poorly Mr. Booth understood that character, admitting that the "laddie did his best, and meant well, still he (MacIlhenny) was the one man living who had got *inside* the part"!

Well along in the season, one of the actors was to

take a benefit, and as he was not much of a favorite with the public, he was greatly worried about arranging an attractive "bill." Perhaps I should say that when one takes "a benefit" the fact is announced on the theatre's bills. The "beneficiary" has the privilege of selecting the play for that special performance, and on that one night, he or she receives one-half, or one-third of the gross receipts of the house, by which he is benefited (perhaps), hence the term, "To take a benefit!"

A couple of weeks before, at the "leading" man's benefit, there had been several volunteers, among them the manager's young daughter, who sang for him, and in MacIlhenny's presence, the worried actor was mourning because there was no one to volunteer to assist him, when up rose Sandy MacIlhenny and offered *his* services. Those who were farthest away writhed in quiet laughter, while those who were near him suffered silently. In that silence the stonecutter read dread of a rival, and he hastened to dispel all anxiety by saying, soothingly: "Don't misunderstand me, young man! You have nothing to fear! I do not ask to play a 'part' in your play — since the public could then have neither eye nor ear for any man but me—and I'd not extinguish any one's light on his benefit—but I'll do a recitation or a reading-like, for you—so 'Put money in thy purse, Cassio,' and not injure your standing as an actor!"

It was a trying moment. They liked the funny, old

chap, and did not wish to hurt his feelings—but good Heavens! the idea of turning him loose before an audience! Again came the voice of MacIlhenny, with the inevitable quotation: "Why whisper you—and answer not, my lords?"

A laugh followed, and the tormented actor asked: "Well, Sandy man, what on earth do you propose to read or recite?"

"Why," answered he, "since you will be doing a tragedy, and I have no wish to outshine you in any way, I'll just give them the "Trial Scene" from "Pickwick."

Through the storm of merriment that followed one or two voices cried: "Let him do it! Let him do it! It will be great!" And just then, at the glass door of the saloon, a tall, gaunt woman appeared. She was one of that body of black-bombazine women who are never ragged, but are always rusty—who all appear of the same age, as they all seem to have passed with reluctant feet their fiftieth birthday. She tapped with a black cotton fore-finger on the glass, and MacIlhenny went to her at once, and spoke with her a few moments —and one exclaimed: "The Two Dromios!" For indeed had it not been for her straight eyes, she might have been Sandy's twin. When he returned some one said: "Your wife, MacIlhenny?"

"Aye," he said, "aye—and though I don't claim she's a beauty, yet 'I'll give no blemish to her honor —none!'" At which they howled with delight, and when they were tired of pounding one another, the voice arose again: "Let him go on—oh, let him go on!" and another added: "Yes, let him go on, just to see how many he'll kill before he gets off again!"

And so it happened that Sandy MacIlhenny, stone-cutter by the grace of God, became, by the cruel whim of man, an actor, and was duly announced on the "benefit-bills" to read the "Trial Scene" from "Pickwick."

Alas, "those whom the Gods will destroy, they first make mad!" It is an ancient promise, and so truly was it kept with this their chosen victim, that on the dark and fatal night that was the beginning of the end for him, poor MacIlhenny saw the radiant dawn of a superb success.

The night came, and a fairly good-sized audience was present. Sandy's reading was placed between the first and second plays, and a more ludicrous figure never appeared before the public. By some mysterious process he had forced his widely bowed-legs into a pair of very narrow, straight-cut trousers. They were of an unsympathetic nature, and as he wore low-cut shoes, they basely betrayed about two inches of white, womany-looking stockings, thus giving a strong suggestion of impropriety to his whole "make-up."

His "wescut," as he called it, he had brought, as he proudly declared, from Scotland, and the actors, as with one voice, had cried: "It looks the part, Sandy, it looks it!"

It was a short-waisted, low-necked vest of a plaid (of course) of red and green and blue and yellow, and the greatest of these was red, and it was velvet, and it had two crowded rows of shining, brass buttons. With quite unnecessary candor, his shirt proclaimed, through dragging wrinkle and straggling band, that it was of domestic manufacture; while an ancient black satin stock nearly choked the life out of him. And his hair—oh, Sandy, Sandy! His wife had curled it on a very small iron, and had then drawn the comb through it, thus setting it a-flying in a wild, red fuzz on whose edges the gaslight glittered, until he looked like some absurd, old Saint with his halo falling off backward!

As this figure of fun appeared, there was a ripple of laughter, and in a few minutes—in the expressive slang of to-day—the audience were "on" to him. The laughter grew and grew—and then that strange *strain* of cruelty, that has come down to us from our ancient barbaric forefathers, and is so much easier to arouse in a crowd than in a single individual, was all alive. They thought they recognized a victim, and they rose to the occasion. They *baited* him; they bombarded him with satirical applause; they demanded certain passages over again; they addressed him as Mr. Buzfuz, and they had just reached the point of throwing things when the reading ended.

As MacIlhenny had no sense of the ridiculous, he could not distinguish the difference between being laughed *at* and being laughed *with*, so it was all like fragrant incense to him, and he came off the stage, his crossed eyes blazing at the bridge of his nose, on each cheek bone a spot of scarlet and a burr on his tongue that made his first words of triumph utterly incomprehensible to those about him. Two of us there were who drew aside, and pitying him, spoke him fair and respectfully, but the others, meaning no harm, carrying on a jest, congratulated him extravagantly, and when he went out from the theatre that night the promise of the gods had been fulfilled, for MacIlhenny was literally mad!

He never did another stroke of work. His kit of tools became strangers to him. He touched chisel and mallet but once more, and that was when he pawned them that he might buy a play-book, and a little bread, with which to quiet for a moment the two devils who tormented him, one gnawing in his brain, the other at his stomach.

In going to and from the theatre I passed the tiny, three-roomed cottage the MacIlhennys occupied, and morning and evening I could hear his high, rasping voice declaiming, ranting, pouring forth pages of old plays, while through the window I could see him brandishing a poker for a sword, and wildly rumpling his little, red flounce of hair whenever he pronounced a curse—whether he was Lear or Richelieu or Sir Giles, it mattered not, he dragged all curses from the roots of his thin, red hair.

Poor Mrs. Sandy had descended from her former

state of bombazine, and was daily seen in black cotton, going out to jobs of washing or office-cleaning, so her neighbors told me. And once, when they missed her comfortable blanket-shawl and noticed that she shivered through the streets in an old Stella shawl, which was a creation of thin cashmere meant for summer only, they rashly spoke the sympathy they felt, and their condemnation of MacIlhenny's course.

It was the first time and likewise it was every other time, including the *last* time they so presumed. She listened in stony silence, and then with bitter pride and icy resentment in every look and word, she demanded: " What else shall my man do ? Is it for the like of him to be pounding stone forever, and he the finest actor-man in all the world to-day?"

Now Mrs. MacIlhenny was a Presbyterian of a blueness like unto indigo, and of a narrowness inconceivable—who have never in her life entered a theatre. Therefore it was but natural that one of the surprised women should ask: " But how do you know that?" And she made answer—oh! loving, loyal, old Scottish wife — with withering scorn and infinite conviction: " Why, has the man na' telled me so hissel'?" and so went her hard way.

For many weeks MacIlhenny had made the manager's life a burden to him—asking, praying, demanding an engagement. " Why, man," he would say, " did you not see the public at my very feet—did you not hear their acclamations, and you know right well that in the absence of garlands and flowers they would have tossed to me anything their hands came upon? What are you afraid of? The enmity of your wee bit stars! I'll see that you suffer no loss!"

Then steady disappointment told upon him. His temper began to change—he grew sullen, suspicious, and began to tell strange tales of being followed at night by certain actors—generally stars. No man could call Sandy MacIlhenny a sponge or beat. When he reached the point where he could not extend a general invitation to those present to drink—he ceased to share in the general invitations of others. And when he could no longer pay his own footing, he no longer entered the saloon, but loitered outside to talk to the actors. Imagining things were not well with him, the actor for whom MacIlhenny had read asked him to accept some payment, but with ever-ready quotation, Sandy refused, gravely repeating: "There's none can truly say he gives—if he receives!"

Then even the outside visits grew far apart, and through my passing of his door I was the only one who knew anything of him, and I knew so little, dear Heaven! so little! Only that he studied, rehearsed, declaimed! I did not know how many, *many* days passed without bringing Mrs. Sandy any job of work, and their pride-sealed lips made no complaint. The old Scotch couple were not unlike a pair of sharp, old razors—perfectly harmless if left alone in their own case, but very unsafe things for general handling—

and so in the midst of plently, they suffered the pangs —the gnawing pangs—of hunger for weary days and wearier nights, and no one knew!

One spring-like day, as I passed the cottage—the window being raised—I heard MacIlhenny's voice at some distance, and recognized the lines of Woolsey in Henry VIII.: "Had I but served my God with half the zeal that I have served—have served—," he stopped—so did I. Some change in his voice held me!" What was it? It was weak and husky, to be sure; but there was something else, some force, some thrill, some strange quality. Again the voice rose: "Had I but served my God with half the zeal that I have served—have served—," almost unconsciously I gave the words, "My King," and he, without even turning his face, took it up, saying "Aye, aye! 'My King—he would not in mine age have left me naked to mine enemies!'" and he laughed. As I hurried on, in all my nerves there was a creeping fear, for in his voice I had felt the subtle difference between ranting and *raving*—had felt the man was mad! And that very morning an actor mentioned him, saying he had seen him in liquor. "Oh, no," I answered, "MacIlhenny never drinks!"

"Well," insisted the actor, "when a man staggers in his walk and talks to himself on the public street, it looks as if he had been drinking too much rye." And another standing by, laughingly said: "Perhaps the old chap has eaten too little, instead of drinking too much!"

Such cruel truths are sometimes said in jest. A few days later, having only to appear in the farce, I was quite late in going to the theatre, and as I neared the cottage, I saw lamplight streaming from its window, and heard Sandy reciting, as usual. But there was some other noise. His words, too, came in gusts and gasps, and I said to myself: "Why, that sounds exactly like two men rehearsing a combat for Richard or Macbeth!" The cottage was flush with the sidewalk and, as I came opposite the window, I could not help looking in, and there I stood and stared, for in the center of the room old Sandy and his wife were struggling desperately for the possession of a hatchet which he held! "Sandy!" she cried, "Sandy!" and all the time Macbeth's lines poured from his lips: "They have tied me to a stake!" Almost he wrenched himself free from her: "I cannot fly, and bear-like, I must fight the course!"

At that moment his wife tore the hatchet from his hand and flung it across the room. He plunged forward to recover it, but in a twinkling she had a grip upon his arms just above each elbow, and next moment she had shoved him into the chair close to the window, and leaning over him, in spite of his writhings, held him tight.

She must have felt my gaze, for suddenly she turned her white face and saw me. Into her eyes there came both fear and furious anger, and then, without loosing her hold for one moment on Sandy's arms, she thrust her face forward, and catching the shade between her teeth, she fiercely dragged it down! And though the rebuff was sharp as a blow in the face, yet for a moment more I stood staring, and saw on the white shade a black shadow-woman bending over and holding fast a shadow-man, and, as a kaleidoscope responds to a touch, at a single movement these shadows blurred, parted, joined again, and this time, though she still held him close, the shadow-woman was on her knees, and her head was on the breast of the shadow-man!—and ashamed to have watched so long, I hurried away and said to myself: "To-morrow I will go there, and sharp words shall not drive me away, until I learn by what route help can reach them!"

Next day I stood and rapped and rapped, but no one answered to my rapping. The house was very quiet, the room seemed empty, but when I carefully looked I saw a little smoke rising from the chimney. The following day the shade was down—I saw no smoke—but I was obstinate, and I went around to the back door and knocked there, and was instantly met by a white-faced "fury!"

"So," she cried, "you have come to spy for them! Well, take them the news! Their work is done! They have no one now to fear—he's gone! He that was greater than them all! Come!" dragging me by main force into the room and to the bed-room door: "See for yourself how he lies there, dead of slow starvation!" One forced glance I gave at the long, long, rigid outline on the bed, but even that forced glance caught, mockingly peeping from under the dead man's pillow, a yellow-covered play-book.

Wrenching myself away from the sight, I turned, and putting my arms about her trembling, old body, I held her close and said: "Oh, you poor wife! you poor, poor wife!"

She stood within my circling arms quite still for an instant, then suddenly her hard face broke into convulsive weeping. She thrust me from her, gasping: "Don't—don't! I say!" and fled to him, while I rushed from the house bearing my ill-news.

Every one was shocked, and one was wounded, that Sandy had not asked his help. He did not understand the sturdy pride of the old pair who accepted nothing they had not earned and asked of the world but one thing, and that was a decent privacy to suffer in.

Three of the actors went at once to the house, the one who had felt hurt, a gentle and kindly soul, acting as spokesman. They offered help to her and burial for Sandy, but they were met with such invective and imprecation as fairly stunned them, and though, by their secret help, they later on saved poor MacIlhenny from the Potter's Field, they were compelled to beat a retreat before his frenzied widow.

With bitter scarcasm she invited one to enter and "bring a brush and see if he could find in that house one crumb of bread!" She told them exactly "how many weeks a man could live upon a kit of tools pawned one by one;" she reviled them as "thieves" for stealing her husband's "great thoughts and ideas of acting;" jeered at them for "cowards," that they had not "dared to stab him," though they had dogged his steps with evil intent many a dark night;" hailed them as "hypocrites," because they hid their joy and, pretending grief, came here and offered "decent burial"—and as they slowly withdrew, she stood upon her doorstep and called after them: "Hypocrites! hypocrites! You starved him to slow death—and he was broken-hearted!"

The word seemed to catch her own ear. She paused —slowly she repeated, "broken-hearted!" Then suddenly she caught the clue—flung her gaunt arms wide —she lifted her tortured eyes to the sky, and with a burst of bitter triumph, cried: "But a broken and contrite heart, O God, shalt Thou not despise!"

And hearing that splendid declaration—that so thrills with hope!—those who had all unintentionally worked her woe, bowed their heads and breathed a quick—Amen!

John Hickey: Coachman

John Hickey: Coachman

"This is to certify that the bearer, John Hickey, five years in my employ, is as honest a man as ever strode a horse.

"(Signed), McDowell, General."

The bearer, John Hickey, stood tall, straight and uncovered before me, while I read the above recommendation. There were several others, but I never looked at them. I knew something of "McDowell, General," in California, and I was persuaded that a man who served him for five years possessed something more than "honesty" in the outfit of his virtues.

But he had, in my opinion, received a still better recommendation at the very moment of his coming into our lives, on that bright summer morning. I had been sitting on the front porch, with a dog on each side of me—that being my usual allowance. Both these dogs—Maida and Sancho—yearned with a great yearning to exterminate the whole race of organ-grinders. They also had a profound dislike for that rather large body of men and women who move back and forth on the earth's surface carrying bundles. Therein lay their only fault; otherwise, they were good, honest, self-respecting dogs. And it must be admitted that this peculiarity of theirs helped to keep things lively about the place and our blood in quick circulation. Therefore, when John Hickey entered the gates, carrying an unusually large valise, there was a roar and a rush before I could form one word of command or entreaty. The blazing eyes and white, uncovered fangs of the dogs told so plainly of their fell intention of reducing him and his valise to a condition resembling desiccated codfish, that any one might have been frightened. But before they reached him I heard a calm voice, and an unmistakable Irish one, saying: " Well, well! What is it now? What is it?"

Lightning could not have stopped them quicker. Their heads lowered, their tails sagged down in a shamed sort of a way. They stretched their heads out and sniffed him a moment. Then, with a wild yelp of joy, Sancho, with slavering jaws, bounded at his breast, striking staggering blows by way of welcome, while Maida, the fierce, was standing erect on hind legs at his side, kissing his protesting hands, and digging with both great paws in his side. At last they subsided a little. He stood, showing the traces of their rapturous welcome, while they sat at his feet, and looking into his face, told him, with shining, loving eyes and excited beating of their tails, that he was the very fellow they had been searching for ever since the seal of their puppyhood's blindness had fallen from their foolish, blue eyes.

During the lull the man produced his little packet of recommendations and passed them to me. My husband, returning at that moment, engaged him in a conversation consisting mainly of questions and answers, and that gave me a chance to look at "the bearer, John Hickey." The only Irish thing about him was his voice. He was tall, square of shoulder, flat of back, clear-skinned and ruddy, with good features, keen, light-blue eyes, and brown hair, which he wore in an odd way, parted down the back of his head, and brushed forward and upward toward his ears, which gave him a peculiarly cocky and alert air. There was something in the carriage of his head, the turning out of his feet, the hang of his arms and the position of his hands, when he stood at "attention," that said, as plain as words could say, " Soldier, yes ; ' ex,' if you like, but soldier all the same." I thought that then ; I knew it by night.

I was just going to put a question to him when the sunlight played him a trick and betrayed his poor, little secret to me. In vain, then, the upright pose, the cocky air, and jaunty manner! It must have been some hours since he had shaved—he wore no hair upon his face, and as he stood there the sun shone full upon him, revealing on cheek, and chin, and upper lip, the glittering frost of age, and he stood revealed, an old man.

I felt touched by the bold bluff he was making against Time, and I wished to give him a trial. Therefore, I looked steadily at my lord and master, and, using that great, unwritten language understood and used by every husband and wife on the top of the earth, I signified my desire for him to engage John Hickey, and he, being a man of intelligence and a husband in good standing, replied by the same means: "All right! but I'm afraid he is a bit elderly. Still, if you wish it!" And he told John to come with him and he would show him his quarters and settle about wages, etc. The words were scarcely out of his lips before the dogs were up and leading the way, with waving tails and many backward turnings of their heads. I think I have said the day was very hot, and as the two men stepped from the lawn to the carriage-drive, my husband, finding his hat oppressive, removed it and held it in his hand. Thus it happened that he walked with bared head at John Hickey's side, while he escorted him to his new home. It was a trivial thing to notice, yet there came a time when it was sharply recalled to me.

The new man had not to take the horses out that first day at all, and in about an hour after his installment he sent a messenger to me, asking if I had a large flag, and if I had one would I not send it down to him, the coachman, who promised to take good care of it?

We had a large flag—yes. But what on earth did the man want with it then? There were four good, solid weeks between us and the glorious Fourth of July. What could he mean? Ah, well! let him have it. So the flag, a really fine one, as it happened, to his great joy was sent down to him.

Shortly after that I saw him with a lot of rope and some tools, tinkering, under the active supervision of both dogs, at the old flagstaff standing on the hill which rises sharply at the back of the stable. Later in the afternoon, chancing to glance from the window, there, sure enough, was the brave, old flag, floating free from the top of the staff. And very pretty it looked, too, against the blue sky and above the fresh, green foliage of the young summer-time. Ah, I thought, that's it, is it? But I had not got it all, even yet, for just before dinner I heard an explosion of some sort of firearm! My heart gave a jump, and I exclaimed: "Good mercy! Has the poor man met with an accident?"

I ran to the window. Out on the hill, by the flagstaff, stood John, while through a cloud of smoke the flag came fluttering down just as the red sun sank from view. I understood at last! My soldier-coachman was saluting the flag, and firing for a sunset gun a rusty old blunderbuss that was likely to kick him through the greenhouse every time he touched it.

I confess I sat down and laughed hysterically. He had intended to greet the rising sun in the same manner, but as sickness in the family required quiet at that hour, he contented himself with simply running up his flag at exactly the proper moment. And when my husband, either from secret sympathy with "Old John's" feelings, or from a fear for the safety of the greenhouse, gave him a good musket and enough ammunition for a modest sort of battle, John Hickey, coachman, was proud and happy.

And so he entered upon his life with us. We spoke of hiring? In our dull way we for some time believed that we had engaged or accepted him, not at all understanding, till much later, that he had accepted us, and that the house was his, the place was his, the fruits thereof, and that the family were his—his household gods—whom he loved devotedly, and served faithfully all the rest of his life.

We were quick to discover that in "Old John" we had an excellent servant and an eccentric man, while the slow years piled up proof upon proof of his loyalty. He won my heart at once by quickly learning the individual characters of our horses. One in particular, my favorite saddle-horse, I was a bit anxious about, since he was getting the reputation of being ugly. He (Creole by name) was a big, spirited Kentucky horse, with an exquisitely tender mouth, requiring a very light as well as steady hand. Two or three great fellows, with sledge-hammer fists, had tried to ride him on his bridle, instead of on his back, and he had, as the result, lifted them not too gently over the top of his handsome head, and they raised the cry of ugliness, when he had simply acted in self-defense, as would any other Kentucky gentleman.

But when "Old John" returned from exercising Creole for the first time, he remarked: "Ah, he's a fine fellow; he's got a mouth as tender as a baby's, and a heart as bold as a lion's. I will be glad to see you on him, ma'am."

John loved the horses as much as people love their children. When he came to us the horses were most all in their prime, but as the years crept by they aged and weakened together, and I was always amused, albeit touched as well, to see "Old John's" fervent efforts to prove to the world that they still preserved all the nerve, vitality and fire of youth. And when the time came when the carriage-horses ought really to have been replaced, "Old John" was a sorrowful man and an anxious one; and at our faintest suggestion of a change, with frowning brow and trembling lips, the old man would march stiffly off to the stable, where he would assure its occupants that "they were mighty fine horses, and people ought to know it by this time."

Like most people of affectionate disposition, he was very fond of keeping anniversaries. All high-days, holidays, and birthdays were precious boons to him, but they came to be occasions of more or less anxiety to the family, owing to his utter inability to express his joy without the help of an explosion. It would seem that the comparatively harmless running up of flags, backed by explosions of varying degrees of heaviness, would be a sufficient outlet for any man's joy. But John Hickey had still a "card up his sleeve," so to speak, for the climax of his love and enthusiasm, the actual perfect flowering of his joy could only be attained by the aid of blazing tar. A great bonfire of wood was not to be despised, but tar was the material worthy of his attention, and when he had diligently sought for and found the most dangerous possible places, and had put in each a kettle of flaming tar, and could gallop wildly back and forth from one kettle to another, trying to prevent a general conflagration, he was the most perfectly happy man I ever saw.

Not more than ten minutes after his discovery that my birthday fell on Saint Patrick's Day he was at the house, asking if the ladies wouldn't let him have some "grane material." That seemed a very vague order—"grane material"—leaving such a wide margin for speculation as to what kind of "grane material" he meant. But the only information he would give was that he just wanted "grane material, dress goods or the like."

Thereupon my mother gave him a deep flounce of all green silk, taken from a retired stage-dress of mine. This he ripped, and pressed, and sewed at, till, lo! on Saint Patrick's morning there fluttered from the flag-staff a brilliant, green silk flag, and I was informed it was there in my honor, not Saint Patrick's. In the years that followed I was very rarely at home on my birthday, but no matter how far away I might be, early on Saint Patrick's morning the green silk flag ran swiftly up the staff. "But mark this now," as he himself would say, never even in my honor, never once did that green flag fly above the "Stars and Stripes." Honest, old Irish-American that he was, the flag he had served with arms in his hands was the first flag in the world for him, and had to take the place of honor every time.

So thoroughly did he identify himself with the family that when anything particular was going on, he, without invitation, yet equally without the faintest idea of presuming, always took his share. On one occasion "Old John" learned that I was expecting a visit from my husband's mother, and hearing me speak of the freshness of her looks, the brightness of her mind, and her extreme activity as something remarkable in one of her advanced years, his interest was at once aroused. Knowing his ways as well as I did know them at that time, I suppose I should have bridled his fine, Irish enthusiasm; but, truth to tell, I was so busy with my own joyous preparations for her welcome coming that I gave no thought to the possible doings of my eccentric coachman. Mamma H—— had heard much of him, and was amused by his stately salute to her from the box. As we entered the gate we met welcome No. 1, in the form of a great flag flying from a staff in front of the house, a thing which had never happened before, and never happened after that visit. Then "Old John" drove down to the stable, while we ascended the stairs, to be met at the top, where we had the least breath to bear it, with welcome No. 2, in the shape of an explosion so heavy that it shook the color out of the cheeks and the breath out of the body of the welcomed lady. Seeing her, after two or three desperate gasps, recover the breath which had been literally shaken out of her, we looked at one another, and all exclaimed together: "John Hickey!" Then she understood, and falling into a chair, she spread out her hands on its arms, laid her head back, and laughed—laughed till the tears came. When she could speak again, she remarked: "What a nice, kind old man, to take so much trouble on my account—but he is a bit noisy, isn't he, dear?"

In his preparations for this visit "Old John" not only shaved himself so closely that he must have removed several layers of cuticle along with his beard, but I had a suspicion that he had shaved the cobble-stones about the stables as well, so shining clean they were, and so hopeless was it to search for a blade of grass between them. Everything was in precise order down there, and I guessed at once that he wished, himself, to show our guest about his domain. At that time he had received an injury—was very lame, and secretly suffered greatly. I say secretly, yet we knew all about it, but it was such a shame and mortification to him to have his condition noticed or spoken of that we all mercifully pretended ignorance at that period of his troubles. When, therefore, we went forth for a morning stroll, and were showing Mamma H—— about the place, I was not surprised to see him hovering about, watching for a chance to capture the guest, and the way he did it was very neat. There was a tiny gutter down there; it must have been fully six inches broad, and as we approached, "Old John," tall and straight (what suffering that forced straightness cost him Heaven only knows), stepped quickly forward, and with impressive politeness helped the lady across—the gutter being perfectly dry at the time. But observe, this action placed him instantly in the position of escort and guide. We all recognized the fact, and took up second fiddles and played to " Old John's " first.

Perhaps I am sentimental, but to me it was rather touching to see how quickly these two old people recognized each other—one a lady born, the other brought up to servitude, but each touched with the fine mystery of old age. With all her gentle dignity, he knew she took a real interest in him, and he gave her a passionate gratitude for her evident comprehension of the pains and penalties time exacted of him. On her part, she saw at a glance the honesty, the courage of the man, and his great, kind heart, and knew him to be as innocent as a little child of intentional presumption—knew that his forwardness was the result of his loving desire to do something to give pleasure to the family. And so it came to pass that they paced about here, there, and yonder—he showing her the horses, the framed pedigrees of my little dogs, two or three wonderful lithographs of myself (all framed at his own expense), and finally presented her with a receipt for a certain liniment for a shoulder-strain in horses, and, having completed the round, he brought her back to us with great pride and dignity.

I never knew a man who loved flowers with such tenderness as did this queer, old coachman. His garden, principally laid out in lard-pails, tomato-cans, and an occasional soap-box, filled my heart with envy by its astounding mass of beautiful bloom. Even the gardeners used to grunt unwilling admission of his wonderful luck. 'Twas all fish that came to John's net. Sunflowers or daisies, lilies or morning-glories, pinks or japonicas—everything he could beg, buy or pick up—he so craved, so longed for flowers. As a chicken will rush for a crust of bread, so would " Old John " rush when sick or dying plants were cast from the greenhouse. He always gathered them up and carried them out of sight, to make his examinations in private and decide upon the course of treatment necessary. A bit later he could be seen, happy and perspiring, filling yet another lard-pail with leaf-mould, etc., a big dog on each side watching with restless, inquiring eyes each movement, and sniffing with infinite curiosity at every article used, while John worked on and conversed affably with them all the time about the nature of the plant and his hopes for its future. One of his great successes was the wonderful restoration to life and opulent beauty of a pair of castaway begonias, almost leafless, entirely yellow, and sick unto death. They were thrown out bodily, and when " Old John " picked them up he was greeted with a roar of laughter from the gardener. The old man was nettled, but he only remarked: " Suppose ye wait a bit now, and by-and-by I'll be laughin' with ye—perhaps."

A long time after, as he helped me dismount one day, he asked me "wouldn't I go down to his room a minute, he wanted to show me something."

And there, in riotous health and beauty, stood two rarely fine begonias, presenting a mass of foliage and a prodigality of bloom only to be found in "Old John's" garden. I was frankly envious, to his great pride. One plant was loaded with great, coral-like clusters. The other dripped clear, white, waxen blossoms from trembling pink stems, and wore such an air of united purity and abundance, that, almost without thought, I exclaimed: "That flower should be dedicated to the Virgin Mary!" John gave me a startled glance, and said, "Why-y-y, why, madam! you're a Protestant!"

"Well?" I asked, "and because I am a Protestant am I to be denied the privilege of loving and honoring the immaculate mother of our Lord?"

Now, I had long known that there was something wrong between my poor, old chap and his Church—the servants declaring that he was no Catholic, or even that he was an unbeliever. "Old John Hickey?" Why, Catholicism was born in him! It was in the blood of his veins, in the marrow of his bones. No matter how harshly he might speak of his Church, nor how long he might neglect his duties, almost unknown to himself, down in the bottom of his heart the old faith lived, warm and strong, and it only needed an emergency to make him turn to the Mother Church as trustingly as a babe would turn to its mother.

I found that "Old John," in his fancied quarrel with the Church, had suffered cruelly. He had neglected his duties, and had then been unhappy because of that neglect. He was very bitter and deeply wounded, and that day he exclaimed sadly: "It's hard, madam—it's hard that a man should be made to lose his soul!"

"Never say that again, John!" I cried. "There is just one man created who can lose your soul for you, and that man is John Hickey!"

He looked at me a moment, then putting one forefinger on my arm he asked, solemnly: "Madam Clara, are you talking as a Catholic or as a Protestant, now?"

Laugh I had to, though I saw it hurt the poor, bewildered one before me and belied the tears in my own eyes. But I made answer quickly: "I'm speaking neither as Catholic nor Protestant, but simply as a woman, who, like yourself, has a soul, and does not want to lose it! Don't look so unhappy! Your Church is beautiful, great and powerful, but there is One who is greater, more beautiful and more powerful. In all the ages there has been but One who left the unspeakable joy of Heaven to come to earth to suffer and toil, to love and lose, to hope and despair, and finally to give up His perfect life to an ignominious death, because His boundless love saw no other way to save us from the horror of eternal death! He paid too great a price for souls to cast them easily away. There is but one Saviour for us all, be we what we may! There is but one God whose smile makes Heaven. We travel by different paths—oh, yes! We wear different liveries, some showing the gorgeous vestments of the stately Catholic, some the solemn drab of the Quaker, others black robes. But the paths all lead to the one place, and the great questions are, do we love the One we seek, and have we loved and helped those we traveled with? John, make Christ your Church, and the mightiest cannot harm you!" and, catching up the scant fold of my riding-habit, I turned and fled from the only sermon I ever preached in my life, while from behind me came certain familiar sentences, such as, "Yis, yis! Ye're fine horses, that ye are, but it's too soon for water yit, y'r know, because," etc., etc., but all spoken in so husky a voice it might have been a stranger's.

Anxious, economical old body, from the early fall he began to watch over the welfare of our house. We, sleeping in it, knew no sooner of a loosened shutter than did "Old John," who immediately began a still-hunt for the offender. But his drollest habit, I think, was the making of a slow, close search over all the grounds, and even out into the road, after every storm, seeking for possible slates torn from the roof. On one of my homecomings from a long season he met me with a small bill for mending the roof, and he anxiously explained that he did it, he knew, without orders, but if he hadn't, it would have got worse and made a leak and would have ruined thousands of dollars' worth of beautiful frocks up there! Please bear in mind that the figures mentioned are "Old John's," not mine.

I assured him it was all right. I thought his face would clear, but no, not yet. He carefully produced a large, flat package from under his table, and when the package was gravely opened, there lay a collection of broken slates. John had saved them all as his witnesses, and he would take up the best of them and explain: "If it had broken this way, instead of that way, it might have been replaced, but as it was, do you think now, ma'am, that I could have done any different?" The second assurance satisfied him, and his face resumed its usual contented look.

So we all moved our wonted ways until that lovely spring day, when a pale-faced messenger ran up to the house to say, "Oh, madam! Old John has had a fall, and he's hurt bad!"

I thrust my feet into a pair of bedroom slippers, being myself ill at the time, flung a loose gown about me, and, with my mother, hurried with all possible speed down to the stable. He was stretched out—not sitting—in a horribly unnatural position on a chair. His face was ghastly, his eyes dim, his pulse almost unfindable. I gave him a stimulant, praying inwardly that I might not be doing wrong. I learned from the others that he had washed the pony phaeton, and was pushing it backward to its place when he had slipped and fallen heavily, face forward, on those cruel cobblestones.

I was convinced he was seriously injured, and leaving my mother attending to his wants and directing the men how to get him to his room, I hurried back to the house, wishing at every step that my husband would come, and hastily telephoned for the doctor. When the doctor and Mr. H—— were both on the spot and I could retire to the background, I was surprised at my feeling of profound depression. "Old John" had had two falls far and away worse than this one, but that look on his face, it was neither age nor pain— though both were there—that so impressed me. It was a look of hopeless finality, and accepting it as a warning, I hastened to inquire if John would see a priest, and lo! as I had thought, the old faith was warm within him, since he answered readily that he'd see the priest, if we would be so kind.

But here the doctor interfered, saying he should prefer the patient to be kept quiet, and to my eager protest made answer: "He is really safe for the night; the morning will tell whether he is fatally injured or not, and I promise I will give you ample notice."

And so I opened my ears to reason, and shut them hard and close against that still, small voice that cried, "Send! send!" and kept repeating the two words I had seen written upon that stricken, old face: "The end! the end!" In a conflict between reason and instinct I have always found instinct to be right, but, alas! I yielded to reason that time.

Down in "Old John's" room all had been arranged for the night. The gardener was to sit up for the next three hours, then my husband would come down and watch the rest of the night. To the patient this was an arrangement of such outrageous impropriety and so exciting that it had seemingly to be abandoned. The lamp was shaded carefully, an open watch lay on the table by the medicine-bottle, glass and spoon, and all were neighbored by a pitcher of lemonade.

Lying on the floor at the foot of the bed was the great dog John had reared from puppyhood, and in the corner, in the seat of the old rocking-chair, three calmly-confident cats lay sleeping. It was all so quiet that when the sick man spoke even his weak tones could be heard plainly.

"Mr. H——, will you be thanking the ladies for their goodness to me, and if you please, sir, could me room be made proper-like before either of them might be looking in to-morrow?"

The promise was given. Then, after a moment, he said: "If you please, sir, would yer be asking the man to keep the door ajar a bit through the night, that the dog might have his freedom? Yer see he's used to it, sir."

This promise also was given, and John lay quiet for some minutes. Suddenly his face became troubled, and once more he opened his weary eyes, and looking up at his long-time employer, he anxiously asked: "Sir, has any one had the sense to bring down the flag?"

And said employer, knowing nothing whatever about it, but anxious only to quiet the patient's mind, answered, "Yes, the flag is down," though at that moment it was hanging limp at the staff.

"John, would you like a drink of water?" asked my husband, finally.

"Yes, if you'll be so kind, sir." (Pause.)

"Do you wish for anything else, John?"

"For nothing in the world, sir." (Another pause.)

Then after a faint movement or two: "Sir, perhaps you'll be kind enough to help me raise my right hand?"

The heavy, nearly helpless hand was raised and laid gently across his breast. He gave a sigh of seeming contentment and closed his eyes.

"Is that all, John?"

"That's all, sir."

"Good-night, then, John!"

"Good-night, sir!" he tenderly replied.

And my husband turned and walked quietly out of the room, to make his report to me, who, anxious and foreboding, was awaiting him. At the lifting of "Old John's" hand I burst into tears. Ah! I thought, he needed no man's help to lift that brawny right hand of his when he swore allegiance to the Constitution of the United States, or later when he took the solemn oath that made him a soldier under that beloved flag, beneath whose folds he now lay, old and broken! And even as the thought passed through my mind, a handful of pebbles came dashing against the window. We both sprang forward, and looking down we saw the terrified face of the gardener, gleaming white in the moonlight!

In his fright he babbled Scandinavian to us, but

finally dragged from his unwilling throat one English word, "Come! come!"

My husband rushed with him down to the sick-room, and at the moment of their entrance found everything so precisely as he had left it that he felt angry at the man's stupid fright. But before he could speak, three shadowy, gray forms slipped from the room, and the dog rose slowly, giving him a sullen, threatening look, then turned, and resting his heavy jaws on the foot of the bed, he lifted his great voice in one long, dismal howl, and dropped to his place again upon the floor, where he lay half growling, half groaning. Fearing that such a noise would disturb the sick man, my husband hurried to the bedside, and, laying his hand upon "Old John's" head, he stood dumfounded, for from the body he touched life had flown!

It seemed incredible, for he had never moved. His hand lay on his breast just as it had been placed there. His face wore the same look of contentment that had come to it when he had said he wished "for nothing in the world, sir," and later, when he had added, "Good-night, sir!" having, at the same time, bidden "good-night" to life and the world.

So, surrounded by the tender care of the family he adored—in his bed—under the same roof that sheltered the horses he had loved—beneath the great flag he reverenced—with his dog at his feet—quiet, peaceful, dignified, such was the passing of John Hickey, coachman.

We covered him with flowers. Nothing was too good to be offered in this last gift to the man who had walked so far with us along life's highway. I had already ordered mass to be said for him. And then I paid him my last visit. I went alone, and talked to him, as foolish women will talk to their dead, and told him how and why I missed sending for the priest, and while I looked at him, I noticed for the first time what a fine head he had, the clearness of his profile, and above all, the calm dignity of his expression. Slowly, like music, there rolled through my memory certain words of Holy Writ: "He raiseth up the poor out of the dust, and lifteth the needy out of the dunghill; that He may set him with princes, even with the princes of his people."

And I knelt at the coffin's side and prayed for this good and faithful servant and friend. A little later I stood on the porch, and through blinding tears saw my husband a second time walk with bared head by "Old John's" side — a second time escorting him to a home.

So he passed out of my life, but never will he pass from my memory. Though he left us without "warning," and asked for no "recommendation," we cannot complain, since he "bettered" himself in following the summons of the Great Master.

Black Watch

Black Watch

That old, black "Watch" believed himself the general superintendent of John Tyler's "back-wood" farm, as well as the guardian of his family, no one could doubt who noticed his busy self-importance, from the candle-light breakfast till the eight o'clock retirement of the family. Then, only, he felt free to visit the secret repository of the few bones he had acquired, or to take a run down the road, and through the woods, to pick a fight with the only dog of his weight to be found within a ten-mile radius.

I should not like to say, off-hand, just what breed "Watch" represented, but he was black all over—was short-haired, heavy-built, and mastiff-like in head and chest. One ear had been injured in a fight with city dogs, and it lopped helplessly ever after, while the good ear seemed doubly quick and perky by comparison.

Now, it was this faithful creature's clear, brown eyes that were first to discover something wrong about young Mrs. Tyler. I don't suppose he knew she had worked to the breaking point—that five babies, with barely a year separating one birth-day from another, were enough to break the high ambition with which she had begun her life, here in the woods, helping in rough, out-door work, as well as trying to make a comfortable home for her husband. And now, that another little one was expected, her songs had ceased, and often she would, in the midst of her work, stop and stand, with eyes fixed on vacancy, a heavy frown on her face that had always before been so bright and kindly in expression.

"Watch," alone, noticed this. The children were too little, and John Tyler too busy, and the brown eyes would study the clouded face until he could bear his trouble in silence no longer, and he would whimper, and push his cold, damp nose into her hand, but instead of the pat he expected, he several times received a sharp rebuke that made him lower head and tail and retire fully five feet from her, where he sat and rapped out a faint, deprecating "tattoo" on the bare floor with his tail.

Sometimes he would rush out and find his master, and climb up and put his paws on his breast and whine, and look back at the house, and John would say: "What the deuce is the matter, 'Watch'? I don't know what you want!" and the man that "helped" would say: "Oh, he's got something tree'd, I s'pose, and wants you to go help him!"

Then the baby arrived, and John Tyler began to understand that an awful thing had happened. His wife's mind was certainly clouded—she was, in country parlance, "not right," and worst of all she had a mortal hatred for the poor, little new-comer. She could hardly force herself to give it the commonest care, and many a time its wails reached the father beyond the house, and only when he entered would the mother sullenly take the child and care for it. "Watch," though he was the most active of farm dogs, took in the situation at once, and calmly assumed the position of nurse to the detested baby.

Never before had he been known to get on the bed, but now he jumped on it every day and curled himself up beside the little unfortunate, and many a time when she cried he would stand over her and gravely lick her tiny face until she stopped, to stare at him in wonder.

He did not wholly neglect his other duties. He saw to the proper watering of the stock, night and morning, taking a few laps of the water himself, as if he were testing it. He led the horses to the field to plow, or to the woods "to haul," as the case might be, running anxiously ahead to see that the road was clear, and then ambling back to bark at their heels a few times before making a circle about the wagon and trotting underneath it a few minutes, to make quite sure the running gear was all right.

Neither did the two eldest of the children succeed in getting to the small creek flowing at the back of the house, without his companionship, though he knew well he would be sent into the water by them for about a peck of chips, after which they were absolutely certain to try to ride him home. Still, it had been his habit to watch the road closely for any traveling dog, at sight of whom he would rush forth with waving tail, and after due investigation of his quality, would either challenge him to mortal combat, or invite him inside the gate to converse about the state of the roads and the scarcity of rabbits, etc. But when the family trouble began, he gave such pleasures up and turned all his attention to his people.

So the day came when John Tyler was compelled to go to town, a great city now, but then a struggling, little town on the edge of a marsh. He dared not leave his wife alone with the children, so, with great difficulty, he secured the help of a young girl, for a couple of days, and then with a big load to take and a long list of things to bring back for the winter's comfort, he started, and was greatly surprised when old, black "Watch," who always enjoyed his "city" trip so thoroughly, after escorting him with leaps and barks and short rushes at nothing in particular for a half mile, suddenly sat down by the roadside and staid there, regardless of his master's inviting whistle.

Back at the house, the morning work was no sooner done than the "girl" was astonished to see Mrs. Tyler come from her room, dressed in her Sunday gown—a work-basket hanging from her arm—and carrying the hated baby. She briefly announced that she was going to visit her neighbor. The "girl" told her she was not strong enough for such a tramp, but she muttered something about "a shorter way," which frightened the girl into reminding her how many wild animals were still seen in the woods, and Mrs. Tyler had turned such a white, angry face upon her, she had not dared to speak again, but, looking after her, saw her twice drive old "Watch" back, when he tried to follow her.

About one o'clock the Brockway family were surprised to see young Mrs. Tyler at their door, and were amazed when they found the baby was not with her! "Oh," she lightly replied, "the girl was at home, she would look after all the children." In those days, unless the mother died, all babes were reared by the simple rule devised by Mother Nature—hence the pained surprise of these kindly womenfolk at the all-day abandonment of so young a child.

As the day wore on, Mrs. Tyler grew more and more absent-minded, and finally her work fell to her lap, and she sat in perfect silence. Suddenly she clasped her head in her hands, she looked wildly from one face to another, then down to her lap, when, with a shriek, she sprang to her feet, and rushing into the next room began throwing on her wraps, all the time moaning: "Oh, my God! Oh, my God! help me—help me!"

She paid no attention whatever to remonstrances or questions! They begged her to wait—they would harness up and take her home! She seemed not to hear them—only shivered and moaned: "Oh, God help me!" and tore away from them, and out of the house, and one who followed a little saw her break into a run as soon as she was out of sight of the windows.

The women were greatly frightened, and calling one of the men from work, sent him after her. He took down a gun and easily and hastily followed the tracks her feet had left in the soft earth on that damp November day. Presently he came upon her work-basket, abandoned at the point where, by climbing the fence, she could leave the regular road and make a cross-cut through a strip of dense woodland. He frowned blackly as he picked it up, saying to himself: "She must be clean crazy to go through there alone! Why on earth didn't she bring old, black 'Watch' with her? He could bluff four times his weight in wild-cat, fox, snake, or even in bear-skin! But alone and sick! Good Lord!" and so grumbling to himself, but with eye, ear and hand alert, he followed the woman, who still kept ahead of him, until, as he was approaching a sudden glen-like opening in the woods, he was startled by a piercing scream, followed by the agonized cry of: "Oh, my God! help me! help me!" and plunging forward, he came upon Mrs. Tyler, who, in hastily trying to clamber over a fallen tree, had been caught and was held firmly by her clothing, and though she fought madly to free herself, he noticed she never took her eyes, for one instant, from some object beyond him.

Following the direction of her glance—he stood stupefied. Almost in the center of an opening stood one noble, hickory tree, and on the damp earth at its foot lay a small, white bundle from which there came, now and then, faint, hoarse wails of utter exhaustion, while, with sturdy legs planted stiffly astride of the abandoned baby, stood old, black "Watch"—a dog on guard!

From the base of his skull to the root of his tail every separate hair bristled fiercely up. His forehead wrinkled wickedly! His eyes glowed with a hot, red fire, while he drew his lips back savagely, laying bare every tooth he owned in the world.

Just as young Brockway was about to speak, "Watch" half-wheeled about and gave tongue, for the first time, in one snarling, half-strangled bark, and, following the movement of the dog with his eyes, the young fellow, for the first time, realized the true horror of the situation, when in the dense undergrowth opposite he saw a lumbering shape—caught a glimpse of pig-like eyes—a flash of white, sharp tushes, and heard a faint grunt from the brownish-black mass, as its clumsy half-trot carried it into the depths of the forest.

There was one shot sent wild by a trembling hand, and, almost in the same moment, a loud, long r—r—rip, r—r—rip, r—r—ripping of clothing and stitches was heard, and a woman's slender figure went flying across the opening, and Mrs. Tyler flung herself upon her knees, crying: "Give her to me, 'Watch'! Oh, give her to me!"

Yet, before her hand could touch the child, the dog turned upon her savagely, while she, seemingly beyond all personal fear, threw her arms about his rigid neck, pressing her agonized, white face against his black head and fiercely opened, slavering jaws, while she pleaded humbly: "Forgive me, 'Watch'! I know I do not deserve it—and you know just what I meant should happen! But, forgive me, 'Watch,' for her sake! Give her to me, honest, brave, old 'Watch'! I promise you I will love her all my life long!"

He held himself very stiff within her circling arms for a moment, looking hard into her eyes, then suddenly he brightened visibly—gave her one all-comprehensive caress reaching from chin to brow—and gently, cautiously stepping backward, left the piteous bundle within the reach of her hungry hands. 'Watch' first looked across at Brockway and wagged a courteous greeting to him, then he stretched himself, both fore and aft, and yawned great, loud, throat-revealing yawns that went far to show how long a time his muscles and his nerves had been kept taut and on the strain.

Meantime, the first loving kiss, the first sweet mother-kiss that blesses where it rests, had been given, and under cover of the all-concealing, matronly shawl of that period, the baby had established communication with the quick-lunch-counter Dame Nature superintended.

Mrs. Tyler needed young Brockway's help in getting home, after the shock she had received, and at the beginning of their long walk his horror of her was so evident that, in self defence, she told him part of her story, and with such effect that there were tears in the lad's eyes when he tried to realize what those dreadful months must have been—during which she could not recall ever to have seen the sun—could not remember any act of her own doing, all that time— save that one awful act!—was only conscious of one desire—to destroy this child, because its coming would prevent her husband from making the regular payment on the farm, and he might lose it and be ruined—so she watched and waited for a chance to abandon the baby to the wild animals—that she might thus save the farm and family—and he rejoiced with her, as she told of how, suddenly at his home, she had had a loud, rushing sound in her ears, the sunlight had become visible to her, she had looked at her lap for her baby, and then remembered she had left it in the woods to be devoured! How she had run—how she had prayed, and God had been merciful!—and he, Brockway, would not hate and fear her now—would he? and he would not speak of this any more than he could help?—and oh, was not black "Watch" a hero to save her darling's life? But the boy thought she owed a good deal to the condition of the bear. It was fat and sleek—well fed, and therefore good-natured. Had it been rough-coated, thin, hungry "Watch" would have probably given his life—and in vain! And then, at her gasping cry at such a suggestion, he had, with rustic, bashful awkardness, "reckon'd he was a plumb fool at talkin', and would she please just not count that in at all?" and so had left her safely at her kitchen-door, while "Watch," dropping the work-basket he had carried home, escorted the young man a short distance down the road, then, taking a jaunty farewell of him, gave himself up to a careful and thorough smelling of apparently the entire farm and all its implements. Of course it was troublesome, but it was the only trustworthy way of finding exactly what had been done during his absence and that of his master.

Late that night, John Tyler, tired, chilled and anxious, drove home, and was met some distance down the road by old, black "Watch," carrying a lighted lantern, and prancing and plunging about so joyously that the lantern light seemed like some small animal running along the road, gliding under bushes, even darting up tree trunks occasionally in its efforts to escape the pursuing dog. The man was surprised, for he felt that only his wife would have given "Watch" that light, and the surprise was pleasant to him.

Then he unharnessed, watered, fed and bedded down the weary horses, eagerly assisted by "Watch," who seemed to be in absolutely puppyish high spirits. Why, even when he had with such frantic violence declared the presence of a burglar in the far corner where the harness hung and Mr. Tyler was compelled to pull down and show to him the old blanket he was mistaking for a burglar (a thing he had never seen in his life and only heard of from a city dog following his master's buggy the summer before)—even then he was neither humiliated nor cast down, but had, as was his wont, slid into the stall of gray "Billy" (the oldest and best horse on the place), and, standing up by the manger, proceeded, with both paws, to dig for some sort of small game in "Billy's" shoulder. Then the horse laid back his ears, opened his mouth and bit at "Watch," who bit back at him—their teeth sometimes clicking sharply together, to their seeming great delight. And this continued until the low whistle of the man separated the friends and play-fellows, and master and dog went to the house together, leaving the closed stable filled with humble rustic music, the rhythmic, melodious expression of utter content, of comfort won, that is produced by the crunch—crunch—crunch of great, white teeth grinding silvery-yellow oats or crushing the brittle sweetness of the orange-colored corn. Listen! Count! One, two, three, crunch—crunch—crunch, now a long, deep, soft sigh, then crunch—crunch—crunch!

At the house John met another surprise. He had expected to hunt about in semi-darkness for the bread-crock and the butter or molasses, or anything almost, and take a "cold bite," and go to bed, but here was as good a supper ready for him as the limited contents of their very primitive larder would allow, and oh! — crowning grace of an American farmer's meal—it was hot!

Only pork, white, firm, sweet as a nut, crisply and amiably sharing the same small frying pan with the sliced potatoes! Hot "corn-dodger" and hotter coffee! But oh, beyond these comforts there was a look in the wife's hazel eyes, a clear, bright, straight look that shook his very heart—it was so like the good days of the past!

When supper was over, and "Watch" was carefully separating his bits of corn-bread with gravy on them from those bits which had none, and after the manner of his race, eating the best portions first, Mrs. Tyler came to her husband and put one arm about his neck, while with the other she closely cuddled the baby to her side. As John stood looking down on them, he felt it was for him a blessed sight, and bent to kiss her; but she avoided the caress, and hiding her face on his breast, she made a full confession.

Perhaps it was as well that she could not see the pallor of his face as she told of the hours the baby lay abandoned in the woods, nor the drops of perspiration on his brow as she described the bear in the thicket and old, black "Watch's" furious defence of the helpless little one. The silence that followed her plea for forgiveness was for a few moments broken only by "Watch." He had sat bolt upright before them, watching their faces closely with his honest, brown eyes, and now he sniffed and snuffled, as though on the verge of tears, while with persuasive tail he rapped on the bare floor so loudly that one might have mistaken the noise for the nailing down of a carpet.

John raised his big, rough hand and smoothed his wife's hair. The clumsy strokes were given the wrong way, and each one pulled harder and tangled worse, until her brown locks were full of what the children would have called "rats' nests." But the awkward caress was sweet to her, as precious as it was rare. Then he said slowly: "Never do it again, Betsey! No! no! I don't mean that! I mean never worry all alone again.

If you are anxious and troubled about the farm, money, or anything else, for God's sake, tell me all about it, and let me share the worry!" and he kissed her, and then looking down on "Watch," he said, gently: "Thank you, old man."

And then I think he did a curious thing, for you must remember "Watch" was simply a farm dog who had never been taught one single trick in all his life. Yet now, when he thanked him, John Tyler offered him his hand. "Watch," embarrassed and confused, lifted and lowered his good ear rapidly, glanced at the hand, then at his master's face, half-lifted his left foot, dropped it again, and suddenly raising his right, laid the black paw firmly in the extended hand, and gravely, unsmilingly, John Tyler held it a moment and repeated: "Thank you, old man."

Ten minutes later the wooden bar was across the door, the candle was extinguished, and darkness, silence and peace descended upon the little, backwood home.

When I, the writer was a little girl, a very, very old lady used on bright, fair days to lead me down the country road, past many white houses amid their orchards, and point out a great, old hickory tree, and tell me that was the spot where she had, in her madness, left her baby, "who is now Mrs. B——," she would say.

But I always had to hear over again about "Watch," whom, the old lady said, "had scratched and fit, and killed 'chucks and snakes, and taken the children to and from school for eight years after that! And then, one night, he had got up from his mat and come into the bed-room and stood by the bed, and had licked the hand of his master, and had gone back to his mat, and in the morning he was quite dead. Just as if Death knew he could only get him away from us by taking him in his sleep!"

And I would lean against the kind, old lady, and say gravely: "What a pity he had to die before I was born—I would have loved 'Watch'!"

And I love his memory to-day—brave, old, black "Watch"!

Dinah

Dinah

Dinah was not "all things to all men," but she was everything to one small girl, and a good many things to other members of the family. I think I had better say a few words right here about the aforesaid small girl. She was an only child, and so far beyond mere prettiness as to be really beautiful. Quick, clever, and high spirited, the slavish idolatry of her mother had worked her ruin. *Enfant terrible*, she was a burden to herself, a terror to all those about her; except during the rare absence of that mother, when, oh! the pity, the shame of it! the little Marie became obedient, gracious, and charming; as sweetly angelic as she was beautiful.

To the friends of the family she was generally known as "Tyler's vixen," "Tyler's malicious imp," or that "pretty little devil of Tyler's," which seems to throw considerable light upon her every-day manners and behavior. Now, it's almost needless to say that this child's path through life had been simply clogged with toys, foreign and domestic, elaborate and simple, with a strong leaning toward the most expensive in the market. Even from that early period when she had but two desires on earth, one to drink long and deep at nature's fountain, and the other to sleep profoundly, they had forced her to keep awake long enough to choose between a rattle of solid silver, with which she could easily have broken her own wee head, or one of gold and silver and coral; and her anger being great, she rejected both, and clutched at a soft rubber affair with a ring handle, offered by the nurse and positively declined by the mother as too awfully common. And it was at that point I made the small Marie's acquaintance, being led in to look at a baby that was so wise that it had selected a ring-handle rattle, because it knew it would be cutting teeth by and by and would need the ring; at least that's what the nurse said. One can imagine, then, what a veritable army of dolls must have fallen to the share of this so cruelly spoiled child. Creatures whose waxen beauty almost broke the hearts of less favored lookers-on; wardrobes complete and exquisitely perfect—packed in real for true trunks; tiny sets of jewelry — toilet-sets — parasols — fans— charming carriages for these gorgeous beings to ride in; blond, brown, and black-haired dreams of bisque, china, and wax beauty; families—yes, whole families of tiny, Swiss dolls, China dolls—from one scant inch to ten in height! It was maddening, and Marie would, as a wee tot, push away the great, prize doll, so heavy for her little arms, and bury her weary face in the pillow and whimper for—she knew not what! Poor, little, *blasé* baby! Always deprived of the keen delight of wishing for a thing, of the hope and fear in waiting, of the thrill of seeing possibility become probability, and then the rapture of possession!

One day this happened in the presence of a woman, a sempstress, who was sitting by at work. She was poor in pocket, but rich in knowledge of life, and kind of heart, and she cried: "Oh, you poor, spoiled child! If you had a nice, clean rag-doll, such as any workwoman's child may play with, you would, I warrant, get more pleasure from it than from any of these big, hard, silk-clothed ladies that you can't baby or coddle to save your life! I've a good mind—" then she paused, but the weary, little face, turned from the splendid doll in dull dislike, brought her to a determination; she went on: "I'll have to be quick, though, for her mother would never give her consent, never!" So Marie was put to sleep, and the sewing-woman left her proper occupation and worked hard and fast on something else, for this was the day of the creation of Dinah.

And I often ask myself this question: If that woman of bright intelligence and good will, acting under the influence of loving pity for an unhappy child, could yet produce such a blood-chilling nightmare as Dinah, what under the blue canopy of Heaven could that same woman produce if her hand were directed by hate or revenge? Nothing short of an eye-crossing, world-convulsing creation, I'm sure! At all events, I made a picture of Dinah, to show a friend of Mrs. Tyler, and when she looked at it, she had a congestive chill, and it was a good picture too.

Personally, I don't approve of written descriptions of people, because they never describe. See descriptions of lost people given to detectives, where height, weight, and possible age are dwelt on with great particularity, while a large, seedy wart, mounted conspicuously on the bridge of his nose, or a drooping, partially paralyzed lid of the right eye is never mentioned. Then again, though Dinah was no beauty, I felt so much respect for her powers of endurance, her silent patience under most trying circumstances, that writing a personal description of her becomes a painful task. However, if you will go back to your earliest youth (a longish journey for some of us, yes, but one still easily made), and recall the paper-dolls of that period, dolls generally cut from the white margin of the evening-paper by the purloined scissors of that member of the family who most objected to your using them, you will remember those dolls were always cut in very wide paper pantalettes, modest but ugly, chaste but very inartistic—well, if you will, in your imagination, trim off the superfluous width of those pantys, so as to make legs instead, you will have before your mind's eye an excellent ground plan of Dinah's structure.

The linen being doubled, and Dinah being all in one piece, it followed that she had great strength of limb, and never, even during the stress and strain of her hardest years, did she lose either leg or arm. Yet, whenever the spoiled Marie lost her temper, the bisque, wax, and china beauties surely lost legs or arms or eyes, Mrs. Tyler lost her head, and poor Mr. Tyler parted with his hopes of heaven, while Dinah remained whole and still in one piece. When her figure was complete, she was about three hands high and without any sign of blood or race about her. One side of the head having been selected for the back, because it had puckered a little in the sewing, it was carefully but lavishly inked, a plain solid coat of ink behind, while about the brow and temples the ink formed those precise scollops, gracefully termed by the French " waterwaves." Then followed the eye-brows, still of ink, and of fearful and wonderful drawing, and below them— eyes?—oh, yes! eyes of course; what else could there be beneath eyebrows but eyes? But they certainly were peculiar eyes; there was no wearying monotony about them, but rather a pleasing variety. One was, I remember, quite nice and round, and looked to the front in an honest, kindly way, while the other was square enough to have corners, and it looked downward and inward, right into that spot where, if she had had any features, her nose would have been. As to the mouth—I suppose I have to mention it—there was so much of it, but I wish I could be silent; you see, the linen was roughly woven, and here and there a coarse, heavy thread appeared, and when the penful of red ink was applied it touched a coarse thread, which soaked up the ink like a sponge and led straight across her entire countenance. Of course the red ink could not be removed, and the situation and the mouth had to be accepted, though it seemed the more remarkable because of the infinitesimal mouths always given to the dolls of commerce.

As to her taste in dress, only words of praise can be

given to Dinah. Never, never did I see her decked out in silk, satin, or velvet, and only once, in the middle of an oldest inhabitant's coldest winter, did I see her in merino.

She usually wore print or gingham, while her undergarments, numerous and beautifully made, were of a material so coarse and strong as to cause surprise to strangers, but to those who had the misfortune to know the little vixen, Marie, these coarse skirts, pantalettes and chemises, stoutly stitched with about thirty-six cotton, were luminous with meaning, suggesting as they did the dread possibility of *tantrums* on the part of said vixen, Marie.

Dinah was complete save for her shoes, which were already cut from a pair of old kid gloves, and her name. I remember her creator wished to call her Lillian, but with all the wisdom of my five full-fledged years well to the fore, I suggested that it would be well for all of us to leave the christening to Miss Marie, herself. And she of thirty-five years bent her head to my five, and the name of Lillian floated back to the limbo from which it had been so briefly called. As the second shoe was taken up, Marie showed signs of waking, and the newly created one was thrust into my hands, and I was told to go and give it to the little tot. But deep down in my soul I said, "Nay! Nay!" for mark you, I was a canny child, and ten years of life's experiences had been crowded into my five of actual time, and hell and bitter punishments took prominent places in the religion thus far made known to me. I said to myself therefore: "This child *is* wicked, for all she is so pretty, she's *awful*, and if for her punishment she is to be frightened to death by the sight of this nameless thing, I don't intend to be the instrument used in her undoing! So, swiftly I crept to the great crib-bed, and in a moment crept away again, leaving across her stomach, like a hideous nightmare, that "deed without a name," and then I fled to the hall and waited for things, behind the partly open door; wondering which of the little cups and glasses on a stand by the bed, holding cooling drinks, would strike the door first. I waited and watched. Marie's eyes opened, a scowl instantly darkened her face; in a querulous tone she asked, "Is my mamma, home, now?"

The voice of the sempstress answered gently, "No, dear," and a light like sunshine came into her brilliant eyes; she smiled sweetly and asked, "Where's my Cawie?" her name for me, and as near as she could get to Carrie, and then she felt the weight across her, and the moment had come!

She lifted the thing, and they were face to face. The child's eyes opened wider and wider, the pupils dilated, the lids flickered nervously, then came a faint, long-drawn "Oh—h—h!" another pause, broken at last by the announcement, calmly and gravely made, "She eyes, don't fit each other!"

Marie had trouble with her personal pronouns, as well as with her relatives.

Next moment she rolled over and began to scramble into a sitting posture, during which she all unconsciously pressed the doll tightly against her little chest. (Oh, for us, happy accident!) for the next instant, with a shout of surprise and joy, she cried, "Oh, she cuddles, she cuddles!"

Two words which were to become familiar to every member of the family, in the time to come, "She cuddles, and she is Dinah, my peshous! Dinah, always!"

And she who had thought of Lillian rashly exclaimed, "But why on earth, Dinah?"

And received for answer, "Caus', I say so, and caus' my mamma jess hates the Dinah song." A so-called "comic," named "Wilkins and Dinah" that Mrs. Tyler raged at when her young brother used to sing it within her hearing.

So it was pure malice that prompted "Tyler's little vixen" to name her new treasure "Dinah"! Then following that rule of action familiar to all small girls with dolls since before the building of the temple, she turned Dinah upside down, that she might know quantity, quality, and condition of her undergarments, and when she found that Dinah possessed that final charm, that very crown of happy dolldom, the ability to have her clothes put on and off, to be dressed and undressed at will, the measure was full, her joy complete.

She turned her Dinah right side up again and kissed

her fondly. At that sight my short legs basely betrayed me, and I sat down with unnecessary emphasis the deaf might have heard. Instantly the cry arose: "You, Cawie, Cawie, come here and see my 'peshous Dinah'!"

I rose and obeyed. Shortly after, when the "peshous one" had been properly shod, and Marie was dressed for tea, we went forth to walk Dinah; but Marie, recalling the three handsome dolls sitting bolt upright in the parlor, suddenly commanded me to return and make faces at them, "real bad faces, too, for being so stiff and big they couldn't cuddle."

But I suggested that she should wait till the gas was burning, and then let the dolls see Dinah, and with malicious joy she waited. And so began the fellowship between those two. Straight into her warm and tender, little heart the vixen took her "peshous Dinah" and gave her a love that could not be shaken by a mother's angry tears, a father's bribery, or the contemptuous sneers of friends and neighbors—a love that lasted so long as Dinah's self. The effect she produced on people at first sight was remarkable. There was Mr. Tyler, for instance; a good-looking man, very quiet, very gentle and very kind. He never drank, yet the first time he saw Dinah he thought he did, and he was afraid to kiss his wife, lest she should think so, too; and I saw him secretly touch Dinah once or twice, to make sure she was real.

Marie's young uncle, too, he was preparing for college, and though he was gay and full of fun, his conduct was excellent, and he was very strict about Sunday observances, but when he met Dinah he exclaimed: " Well, I'll be d—d ! " Perhaps that was not Dinah's fault. He might have been thinking of his future state, and had just arrived at that conclusion.

Perhaps the most disagreeable occurrence was when the minister, Presbyterian, called, and not having his glasses on, sat himself down heavily upon Dinah. He instantly sprang up to remove the foreign substance he felt beneath him, and meeting the malevolent eye of the " peshous one," he exclaimed, in a startled tone: " God bless my soul!—er—er—I should say—what on earth ? "

But with a bound, the vixen, Marie, was at his side, crying: " How dare you, you too fat, bad old man; you sat on my Dinah and swor'd, you did ! "

With a crimson face he answered: " Oh, no ; oh, no ! my dear little child, you are mistaken. I——"

But Marie stamped her foot at him and cried: " You swor'd ! you swor'd ! " upon which tableau entered Mrs. Tyler.

Gradually, however, Dinah came to be accepted by the family, and it was surprising to see how useful she became to its various members. Mr. Tyler, who did a good deal of office work at home, used her almost continuously as a pen-wiper. Instead of having to pick up a tiny round of cloth and carefully fit the pen to a narrow fold, Dinah allowed a largeness and freedom of movement very pleasant to him. Just a swipe at her in almost any direction, and the pen was clean.

The young uncle, who delighted in the comfort of a rocking chair, yet detested its movement, used Dinah as a sort of brake, placing her under the back of a rocker at just the right angle to prevent action, while many a time the somewhat flighty housemaid, having forgotten to dust the "what-not" (indispensable adjunct of the parlor of that date), would snatch up Dinah and dust all the shelves and their contents with her, fitting her arm or her leg into the depths of "To a Good Girl," or "From Chelsia," or "Friendship's Offering"—these cups and mugs, with their roses and posies and fine gold lettering, being veritable dust traps, as were the sea shells, with the Lord's Prayer cut on their surface, and the parian-marble Rebeccas standing by salt-cellar-like wells, and of such was the bric-a-brac of that day, you know—the day of wax things under glass shades.

The entire family used the back of Dinah's head as a pin cushion, while again and again I have seen her act as an iron-holder, when a sash ribbon or bit of lace had to be pressed just there in the sitting-room.

But it was as a weapon of defence that she got in her really fine work. Grasped firmly by the legs and directed by impassioned energy toward a wisely selected point, Dinah was capable of giving a blow as surprising to witness as it was stunning to feel. Practice makes perfect, and so it came about that that vixen,

Marie's, aim was so quick, so steady and so true, that she landed with Dinah right on the intended spot every time. She paid no attention to rules about the belt line, striking below it with as much vigor as above it. There was never any clinching, because no one would come near enough for that, but I have known her to strike a blow with Dinah hard enough to rupture Mrs. Tyler's agreement with the cook.

Some months after Dinah's arrival I became recognized as a sort of family lightning-rod, since I had the power of deflecting the fluid wrath and deviltry of Marie's temper and leading it to comparatively harmless points.

She was very fond of me, partly because I was older than she was, and partly because I found so many new things for her to play. Everything I saw away from home was served up at once as a play for Marie. Oh, that was a great occasion when I saw a lady faint in a store! Dinah had to faint so many times in one day that she was wet clear through her whole body, from her many revivings, and was in such a disgraceful condition from the brandy we gave her that, being utterly unable to stand, she had to hang on the clothes-line several hours before she could be endured in a warm room, and I remember Marie asked me if the lady had smelled like that.

Mr. Tyler was not a very strong man, not sickly— what a hateful word—but rather delicate; in fact, though he never *said* so, he had nerves, and it must have tried them severely when he came to breakfast and had to face Dinah, sitting in the middle of the table, with her back against the big family castor, and her one straight eye fixed upon his shrinking countenance. The skeleton at the banquet never made half the effect the "peshous 'un" made, for in the first place the skeleton was crowned with roses, and there were bright lights and a small river of wine to help the guests forget the presence of their ghastly companion; but no skull that was ever bleached had a smile to compare with Dinah's, which crossed her entire face and would have gone on and met at the back of her head had it not been stopped by her side seams, where her front and her back were sewed together. There were no roses on Dinah and no wine to dim her effect, and poor Mr. Tyler chipped his egg and crumbled his roll, but, with that eye upon him, got no further, and merely taking his coffee, he fled. The rest of us got a side or back view, so we did not suffer so much. This went on until dyspepsia developed. I have said before, I was very fond of Mr. Tyler, and I began to look for some way to help him. One day, at table, the uncle had nearly betrayed a surprise that was being prepared for the little Marie, and Mrs. Tyler reached out her foot and pushed him to enforce silence, a movement at once discovered by that acute young person, who thereupon made a scene, and thereafter passed much of her time, at meals, hanging head downward from her chair, trying to see under the table that she might (in her own language), " see who kicked who," a habit which caused many upsettings of things and much discomfort, but one to which she clung until I made a suggestion which found favor in her eyes.

"Ah!" said I, "if Dinah belonged to me I'd make her do something lovely!" "Oh, what?" cried the little vixen, and after much coaxing I spoke, with the blessed result that for over two weeks, at breakfast, dinner and tea, Dinah, the dreadful, was carefully placed *under* the table to watch " who kicked who." " Ah!" cried Marie, "yer can't wink yer eyes at each other, 'cause I is looking at yer all! Yer can't kick each other, 'cause Dinah's looking at yer hard, and if yer spell things, I'll—I'll—I'll just hold my breff and die! so now, I'll have to know everyfing!"

But Mr. Tyler ate his egg and toast, and smilingly drank a *second* cup of coffee mornings, and he patted my shoulder and gave me a big, red Canadian penny, which Marie, being jealous, took from me and threw down the well, while the young uncle started the lightning-rod idea, saying "that I had diverted Marie's deviltry from the top of the table to the bottom, where it was harmless."

I will mention one episode in Dinah's life, and that will serve to indicate pretty fairly what the others were like. I always call it the hail-stone episode. Late one afternoon a violent storm had come on. We were all frightened, and poor, little, spoiled Marie was quivering from head to foot with nervous terror. Presently the rain turned to hail, great lumps of ice came dashing against the windows, and "crack!" went a big window-pane, and in fell the pieces of glass. Again came the rushing rain, and the water falling on a table covered with books, the house-maid caught up *something* and thrust it into the opening in the broken window. Alas, and alas! that "something" was Dinah! The "peshous un"! Dinah the beloved! There she was, her cross eyes looking at us from between her glove-shod feet, like a contortionist at a circus, while her doubled body was thrust out into the hail and rain outside. And there, all unknown to us, she remained for a long, long time, and the thunder rolled and the house shook till the spoons rattled and tinkled in their holder. And suddenly Marie lifted up a marble-white, little face, and putting out her hand to my mother, said, faintly, "Aunty? (courtesy title only) tell God, please stop! I'm frightened!"

The awful dazzle of lightning followed her words, and again she buried her face, laying her tiny hands over her ears, to keep out the terrifying sounds. A lamp was lighted, and they began to undress her and prepare her for bed, simply to divert her attention from the storm. She was very silent, but she shook violently, and her eyes were strained and wild-looking. Suddenly the heavens seemed to flame! The crash that followed left the ears ringing! We all cried out, but the vixen gave a bound and stood in the middle of the room; her eyes fairly blazed; she raised them to the ceiling, and in a shrill voice she cried, "Stop! stop, I tell you! I'm frightened!"

Again a dazzle of lightning, again a roar of thunder, and in an instant that little bundle of nerves had darted to the hall, and with both hands succeeded in turning the knob (the wind did the rest), and to our unutterable horror, we saw her little, white-robed figure dart down the steps, and standing on the bit of rain-soaked lawn, mad with rage, she lifted her challenging face to the black sky, and stamping her bare, little foot, she cried, against the wind, "How dare you, God? I'm little Marie Tyler, and I told you I was afraid! How dare you? a great big God like you, frighten a little girl like me?" and then she was in her mother's arms, and was carried into the house dripping as from a river, and spitting and hissing like an enraged cat.

The storm ceased at last, at least the *outer* storm; there was another coming, for where was my "peshous Dinah"?

Every one looked, looked high and low, looked until we got to the place, where we stood and looked stupidly at one another, and then there came, in a strained whisper, from Marie: "What's that?"

She pointed at a dripping bundle sticking in the broken window-pane. Mrs. Tyler screamed outright! Those cross-eyes looking at her from between those stubby feet. There was a wild *abandon* in the attitude that shocked her! But her scream was as nothing compared to the succession of shrieks that broke from the throat of "Tyler's pretty little devil"! "Who? a—a—ah! Who? a—a—ah! Who? a—a—ah!" she screamed after each "Who?"

At last she finished, "*Who* put my 'peshous Dinah' in that hole? She shall be killed, all dead! and put in a hole, her own-self! She shall!! She shall!!!" She caught up a glass from the table and dashed it on the floor, breaking it in pieces. "Hurry! or I'll break everything, I will!!" And when Dinah was pulled out and straightened, words of mine fail to describe her appearance!

Marie held loving little arms out to receive the dripping stop-gap, saying: "We'll go to bed, right now, my 'peshous Dinah'! Never mind your nighty, you'll get cold! Come, and we'll cuddle up, until you are all dry again!" And then the storm broke! It was simple impossible that Marie should be allowed to go to bed with that dripping bundle pressed in her arms, and it was equally impossible to make her obey or listen to reason. It was a wretched scene. The mother knelt to the child she had ruined, calling her, "her angel, her star, her flower," and Marie gave her a kick or a push at each word, and swore oaths that a mule-driver would hesitate before ejecting in a row. Where had she learned them? Who knows? Who ever knows how a beloved child learns evil? But on and on went this battle, until at last, worn out with the past fright and the present rage, the little vixen fainted.

Mrs. Tyler sent for the doctor, and while waiting

his coming, and after Marie's recovery of consciousness, she said to me: "Carrie, can't you think of some way to keep that awful doll away from my darling to-night? Try, child, try!"

I thought hard enough to turn my hair gray, it seemed to me, before I was gladdened by an idea. I went to the door and beckoned Mrs. Tyler, and asked her, in a whisper, two or three questions about an article she had been reading aloud when the storm arose—an article about the water-cure, then the very newest fad. She gave me the desired information, and thus armed, I stole to Marie's side, and with great seeming secrecy, told her I had a lovely new play, if only her mother would allow us (poor Mrs. Tyler!) to play it.

Rather languidly, she answered: "To-morrow, Cawie!"

But I said: "To-morrow would be too late, because Dinah had to be awful wet to play this game."

At once she was all eagerness, and commanded me to explain. And so it came about, that the "peshous un" was stripped under loving eyes and rolled in a wet dinner-napkin, and then "packed" in wet sheets, all according to "Hoyle," or the water-cure doctors. And I engaged to give her several drinks of water during the night, and assured Marie that she would find her "peshous Dinah" all right in the morning, and Marie laughed and talked, while I did the packing. And the doctor found her with a high pulse and red cheeks, but the wet doll was not in her arms. She refused to show her tongue, because she said the last time she put out her tongue at him, he was mad about it, which was very true.

He gave her a powder, she went to sleep, and the rest of us humbly thanked our Creator.

Dinah was snatched out of her "pack" and put in the warm oven to dry, while the other members of the family slept the sleep of the weary and the worn.

Three entire years passed in alternate peace and strife. Acting in the interest of decency and cleanliness, Mrs. Tyler had covered Dinah with fresh linen several times. Little Marie had grown taller, more beautiful, and more impish; while Dinah still reigned supreme, though almost every bureau in the house had in its bottom drawer a wax doll or two, rolled up in towels.

For some time before the great disaster, we had been tormented by cats. Why our garden should have been selected for their mass-meetings, I can't imagine. We lived in a fashionable quarter; there was an air of eternal Sabbath brooding over our heavily shaded street; a few lap-dogs resided thereon, but no one stooped to cats. Yet night and cats descended upon us together.

Mrs. Tyler raised many herbs for kitchen use, but after the arrival of the cats the herbs entered the kitchen no more. The back garden was destroyed.

They were a musical as well as warlike race, and their head notes, chest notes, and stomach notes, were poured forth with passionate ardor, but I never, never learned to distinguish the tenderest love song from the wail of complete despair, though I was quick to recognize the gage of battle. I also learned that the bitterness and ferocity of an engagement was not to be measured so surely by the loss of blood as by the loss of fur.

But let me stop right here, and not weary the reader with what I know about cats—tribal, nomadic, domestic; their habits, laws, and superstitions; their sign-language, being the very same that was taught to the tail-chasing, sacred kittens of Cheops and the first Pharaoh—and only state that in the study of feline folk-lore, I have known of a student becoming so absorbed that he forgot everything on earth, even the " lore," in his mad pursuit of a feline.

Now, one evening, Mr. Tyler brought home an old friend, whom he asked to dine and pass the night. The old friend had with him a small dog, who also dined and passed the night. The gentleman was a bachelor then, and if he is alive and sane, I have the biggest and ugliest silver dollar in the world to bet against a crooked hair-pin, that he is a bachelor now. The dog was small, and it had hair—lots of hair—and judging by sight alone, that was all he had. His master claimed that he could see a difference between fore and aft, between head and tail. Well, perhaps he could when the dog was awake, but 'twas base boasting to make any such claim when he was sleeping. He was named " Bolivar," not after the military gentleman, but in memory of his youthful and almost fatal attempt to swallow whole one of those very large, hard, round candies boys call "Bolivars."

This four-legged guest had made that thing adored of men, "a record," and it was for killing rats. Now you show me a dog with a record for killing rats, and I'll show you a dog who has broken the record killing cats. It's perfectly natural; he has to kill the cats or there would not be rats enough to make a record with.

Bolivar was graciously received by Marie, who knew but little of dogs, and who asked "why he bit his own back when everybody's legs were in his reach," adding, "If I was a dog I'd bite somebody else every time;" which was pure and unadulterated truth, I'm sure.

In the forenoon of that day, "Tyler's pretty devil" had favored us with one of her wildest tantrums. The servant, Norah, had spilled a little hot tea over Dinah's foot, and Marie had gone into a very frenzy of rage. Seizing Dinah by the legs, she had thrashed the girl out of the room and the house; had with one sweep of Dinah's body cleared a small table of every article it held; had cut her own hand; had held her breath until she was blue; had indeed furnished her whole family with healthy but rather unpleasant exercise for both mind and body, and when she had so stirred her monkeys up that we each chattered our teeth while we swang madly from our own particular pole, she had suddenly calmed down and requested me to bandage Dinah's scalded foot, and proceed with her to the garden, there to play "sick lady in the country."

By some chance there had sprung up, at the very foot of the garden, a large weed, a most uncommon growth amid such surroundings; a great, big, coarse-leafed, pinkish-topped thing, a sort of pretty tramp from the woods or fields; I think it's called milk-weed, though to Dinah it was usually an orange orchard, while only occasionally it became a pine forest in which we lost ourselves and endured great hardships.

I remember it was an orange orchard that day, and after a long play, when Marie was called to dress for dinner, she advised Dinah to remain where she was, saying, "When dinner is over I'll bring you some dessert."

So I gave Dinah a book to read, and we left her. We both looked back, Marie many times, and always kissing her hand. And so I most often see her in my memory, the "peshous one," I mean, sitting stiffly against the trunk of her orange tree, one foot bandaged (without the formality of first removing her boot), an open almanac on her lap, whose piteous, gray, old jokes were to entertain her during our absence, her water-waves trim and neat, her round eye mild and pleasant, her smile almost meeting behind — so I saw her that last day.

The dinner was over; it had not been what you might call an hilarious affair. There seems to be something in the blood of wives at enmity with *uninvited* guests, and Mrs. Tyler was cold as ice and as bitter as a black frost.

When dinner was nearly ready, Bolivar sneaked out to the kitchen, where the cook had given him a large, square meal, feeding him from her own hand, as she told me afterward in confidence, until " he was that full his eyes bulged, Miss!" And in that dreadful state he waddled back to the dining-room, and when dinner was over, sat on end by his master and laid beseeching, hypocritical paws on his knee, and was fed again, after which he was in a condition bordering on appoplexy, and quite unfit to play "soldier," or "dead-dog," or do anything in fact, save retire to the flyless shadows under the piano and there sleep, audibly. Marie was so interested in Bolivar and so busy flirting with his master (she was a coquette at one year), that she actually forgot Dinah, who still sat in the orange orchard.

The bare idea of a dog sleeping in her house filled Mrs. Tyler with such indignation that other arrangements had to be hastily made for Bolivar's accommodation.

Some former tenants had left a kennel behind them. It was brought from the wood-house, a bit of old carpet put into it, and the sleepy Bolivar was hitched to it with a piece of cord. After two or three strangling efforts to follow his master, kennel and all, into the house, he finally settled himself, and we all separated for the night.

We were all asleep—and then we were all awake again! No, it was not the "crack of doom" we heard, but if you were to break one boiler factory into a foundling asylum and beat them together, you might get an idea of the kind of noise that aroused us. I murmured "Cats," and tried to slip back into the sweet land of "Nod," but there came a new noise. It had a wooden sound. What was it? My mother said "Is the wood-pile falling down?" But it sounded to me as though the shed was jumping up and down. Suddenly we gasped, "The dog! The kennel!"

Next instant the cord broke and with an ear piercing "ky—i, ky—i!" Bolivar set out to build up another record. It was fearful! The carnage was great, but the noise was maddening. Our nearest neighbor came to his window and made very, *very* personal remarks about people who would keep a dog where they knew cats came. This gentleman's head was like a large, china egg, for baldness, and I think the extreme hairiness of Bolivar added bitterness to his words.

Had Bolivar been satisfied to kill his cats once only, his record would have been bigger, but he had a habit of killing his victims several times, going back to them and shaking and tossing them and crunching their spines with his front teeth, and while this habit had the advantage of making his cats and rats very dead indeed, it lost him a good deal of time.

I slipped out of bed and went to the window and

looked out, just as the triumphant Bolivar tore around the house, dragging his prey and kicking up the grave as he ran. Just beneath me he paused to re-kill his victim, shaking it viciously, tossing it over his head, and with a goatlike spring catching it again. Then, taking it at the head, he, with savage growls, began nipping it down its back. At that moment I heard the stairs creak, and some one softly opened the front door, and then Mr. Tyler's friend came into view.

He was dressed, or—that is to say—er—er, well, he wasn't undressed, quite. His feet were thrust into a pair of heelless slippers, and I experienced a feeling of some surprise at the number of strings I could see dangling from him. There were two broad, white ones hanging down behind from the waist-line, and at least four pieces of white tape trailed along behind his bare heels, which looked in the moonlight like a pair of fine onions—moonlight always has that strange, transforming power.

Yes, though his dress was careless and simple to a degree, still it answered quite nicely for two o'clock in the morning, though ten hours later it would have landed him in the fine, new insane asylum waiting for gentlemen dressed that way.

He conversed with Bolivar a few moments, and his gestures, while a trifle angular, were really very impressive and expressive. What he said seemed to fill Bolivar with utter amazement, and finally with shame and vexation. I am positive that, had he had a tail, it would have been but a wagless sagging down, and vanity of vanities. As it was, he could only bow his head and meekly follow his master, carefully stepping on all four of the trailing tapes, whenever he could, and making a snap now and then at the broad, white things dangling from the waist-line.

Once more was he put into the kennel and tied, this time with a clothes line, which might have tried the strength of the best steer in the cattle market. Once more peace descended upon us. Bolivar had earned fresh laurels to rest upon. The live cats had gone away, and the dead cats kept perfectly quiet, which was all one had the right to expect of them.

It was yet very early morning when I heard Norah at Mrs. Tyler's door, knocking, and crying in a tearful voice for her to " get up fur huvvens sake ! "

She also called upon such a very large number of Saints to come to her help that I am sure the house could not have held them had they laid aside their symbols and things and answered to her call. I suppose they felt that everybody's business was nobody's business, so none of them responded.

Mrs. Tyler was unmistakably vexed as she opened the door, and Norah was unmistakably startled, for Mrs. Tyler not only kept her teeth in a cup of water over night, but, to make it wave, she plaited her front hair in many, many tight, little braids (that was before crimping-pins), which looked like nothing so much as a bunch of nicely cleaned and neatly tied rats' tails.

"What is the meaning of all this to-do?" asked the lady.

"Oh, Mu'm, its all that divil's own dog's doin's! Him that I fed with me own two hands, last night, till his shape was gone intirely! And now she's tored to pieces! The Saints be good to us!"

"Do you know," cried Mrs. Tyler, "what you are saying!"

"I do the same!" replied Norah. "I'm a'saying that that dog 'Bullinger' has tored her to pieces, and she's as dead as any mack'rel!"

"Who is dead, Norah?"

"Why, Miss Dinah, poor thing!"

"What!" Mrs. Tyler stepped outside and quickly closed the door behind her. She took Norah by the wrist, gave her a shake, and asked in a low tone: "What's that about Dinah?"

With a burst of excited tears, Norah repeated: "She's dead, M'um, as dead as any of them nasty cats down there! And I thought I'd come and tell you, M'um, and if you please, M'um, before the young lady finds it out, I'll just be leavin' me place! No M'um, you needn't give me no character! I'll just be goin' peaceable-like, without any character at all!"

And long and earnest were Mrs. Tyler's entreaties, and many were the promises she made of protection from the wrath to come, ere Norah could be induced to light the kitchen fire, her first unwilling step toward getting breakfast ready.

Then, white and trembling, Mrs. Tyler called my mother. They went forth and saw Norah had told the truth. They returned and held a consultation. Mrs. Tyler was for mad haste and another Dinah! Mother was positive the deception could not be carried out on such short notice, and a discovered attempt would add fury to the storm.

But Mrs. Tyler insisted, and together the two women worked wildly, in the hope of recreating Dinah. With dripping brows and trembling fingers they were fastening on her boots, when shrill and clear came the cry of "Dinah! Where's my peshous Dinah? I want her!"

Truly we all wanted her at that moment!

I was scrambling into my clothes as fast as I could, when through the open door I caught a glimpse of little Marie; the next instant there was a cry of indignation, followed by the words: "What's that? What ugly fool thing's that—dressed up just like my Dinah? Who's been here already?"

And Mrs. Tyler tremulously cooed that "No one has been here, darling—it is not even time for breakfast yet."

Marie, with curled-up, contemptuous lips, held the intended deceiver out at arm's length and slowly and derisively put out her spiteful, red tongue at her — then suddenly caught her by the heels and hurled her out of the window, remarking: "You nasty, little, ugly beast! I hope the 'hoppers and the ants 'll get all over you, and fleas in your stockin-legs, too! And who ever brought you here shall be pinched, all black! So there! Now, where's Dinah?"

A pretended search followed, till suddenly Marie remembered she had left Dinah out in the garden. "Oh, Cawie! Cawie!" she cried, "I forgotted her, my own, peshous Dinah, and she's been reading all night, without her dinner! Oh, Dinah! Dinah!" and away she started to the porch, on her way to rescue her beloved. And then the old struggle, between mother and child was renewed. In her foolish endeavor to deceive Marie a little longer, Mrs. Tyler told falsehood after falsehood. Now it was a curious thing about the vixen, that she was utterly truthful, for her mother was a prolific, though inconsequential liar— her lies so utterly lacking cohesive power that they never were known to sustain one another, and Marie often berated her mother for her wrong-doing.

Now nearly distracted, the child suddenly turned to me, asking: "Cawie, Cawie, has my Dinah fallen down the well?"

I shook my head, and answered, "No, Marie, dear," while in the same moment Mrs. Tyler quickly exclaimed: "Yes, my sweet, she is in the well, but the man will get her out, and tomorrow you shall have her in all new things!"

Marie glared at her a few seconds, then stamping her foot, cried, "How dare you, you so wicked mamma! Stop, now! Stop, I say; you make lies every day, you do. Go do your hair up right, and sit in the parlor and make lies, and let me find my dear Dinah. Cawie, will help me!" and as she got through the door and into the dew-wet garden, Mrs. Tyler cried out: "She's all right, she is in—in—the oven getting dry. You can have her soon, only my angel, come and get dressed now!"

But, with a cry of delight, her angel tore out of her hands and darted into the kitchen, and before Mrs. Tyler could signal, much less speak to Norah, Marie cried: "Norah, what's in the oven?" and that honest bond-maiden answered, "Nothin', Miss, its not hot enough for biscuit, see!" and she threw open the door, and into its black maw disappeared the child's bright hopes. She stood quite still, and looked first at one and then at another. I was crying quietly, but I watched her and saw her face growing paler and paler. At last she took a fold of my mother's dress in her hand and said: "Auntie, is my Dinah dead?"

Before she could lift her bent head to answer, Norah, with a mighty roar, burst forth: "She is, Miss, she's dead and killed, and all tored up, and there's nothing left of her!"

Poor, little soul! Both hands clasped convulsively. That curious quiver came to her eyelids, and the movement in her slender throat showed that she swallowed dryly at something—sorrow is always so hard to swallow! Then she flung out her arms, and giving a cry that pierced like a knife, she flung herself out of the kitchen, and, of all places in the house, made straight for the dark store-room, off the dining-room; she who feared but two things, lightning and utter darkness, now sought the latter, and closed the door behind her, where we heard her little hands feeling for some catch or bolt to fasten it, but luckily, there was none. Mrs. Tyler was nearly wild; the pantry was very small, utterly dark, and nearly airless. In it were kept barrels of flour and sugar, boxes of tea and bags of coffee, and closed, it was black as night. She prayed, pleaded, flattered, promised, and to each prayer came a kick at the door, and the threat, "If you touch the door, I'll make me dead! I will! I will!"

Everyone stood helpless before this small child's power to harm herself. Mrs. Tyler denounced Norah for telling. Other members of the family begged at the door to speak to Marie a moment, just a moment, in vain; yet her voice was distinctly weaker, and all were frightened.

"I must bring her out by force!" declared Mr. Tyler.

And then, for the last time, I was called upon to play "lightning-rod." The uncle said, "Let Carrie try," and then all hands were on my shoulder, pushing me forward, and before I knew it I was alone. I on one side of the door, stupid and idealess, and Marie on the other side, heartbroken and relentless. I was quite a big girl then, but I'm afraid I had my finger in my mouth.

I tried to think, but I didn't; on the contrary, I discovered a little nail-hole in the door that had been filled up with putty, and then, faint and low, almost in a whisper, I heard, "Oh, Cawie, Cawie! Oh, my Dinah!"

And I sprang to the door, opened it, and went in, and the next instant I was sitting on a bag of salt, and poor Marie was across my knees, sobbing as though her heart would break. I had left the door part way open, and as I heard some one cautiously approaching, I wildly waved my half-laced boots at them to keep away. I had not said a word; I only sat smoothing her silky, auburn hair, while she cried, and cried, and cried, and every now and then gasped, "She's gone, all gone, every bit of her! Oh, my Dinah!"

But when she once added, " and I can't do anything for her in the world," my idea at last arrived, hurried, out of breath and belated, but still an idea, and I eagerly said, "Oh, Marie, dear, there's a little of her left, enough to make a beautiful funeral!"

She shook her head, saying, "Got to have their bodies to make funerals."

"But," I went on, "don't you remember the poor men your papa saw all blowed up by the engine? There wasn't much left of them, but they had funerals, every one of them."

She turned her tear-wet face toward me, and asked, dully, "How much was left?"

"Oh," I replied, with an airy assumption of knowledge worthy of my elders, "bits of skin, and little bones like teeth, you know, and broken 'spenders.'"

"But," objected Marie, "Dinah's teef hadn't *growed* yet, and she didn't *wear* spenders," and her sobs broke forth anew.

I reassured her by telling her there was quite a large piece of Dinah's flannel petticoat left, and over half of her face (including all of her indestructible smile), and perhaps we might find some more bits if we looked, and we could put them all in a little, white sheet, in a true box (a wooden box), and truly bury her just like any other person.

The poor, little vixen sat up and put her hair from her eyes and listened—she began to be interested—then the tears slipping down her wan cheeks, she stole her arm about my neck and whispered: "Cawie, where has the *inside* Dinah gone?— the— the now-I-lay-me-down-to-sleep Dinah?"

I was silent; and I could feel the trembling of her body increase as she waited for an answer. Then she wailed: "Oh, Cawie! tell me! tell me!"

Poor baby! who wanted her doll to be immortal as herself! I dared not say she was in Heaven, so without an idea of what Paradise meant, I calmly told her that "Dinah was in dolls' Paradise"—and that was the only time I ever knew her to be called a doll.

"What's that?" asked Marie, eagerly.

"Why," I answered, "it's a lovely, clean, sweet

place, where dead dolls wait till their owners get dead too, and call for them on their way to Heaven."

May I be forgiven—but I certainly had a fine, able-bodied imagination in my youth.

"Oh," cried Marie, and she put her little lips to mine and kissed me sweetly, "Oh, Cawie! I'se glad, and I do hope she won't get out and get lost—she gets lost very easy, you know—before I get dead and go for her," and she took my hand and we came forth from the store-closet, and at sunset, in a deal-box with brass hinges and lock (from the young uncle), in a white, silk handkerchief (from Papa), Dinah's scrappy remains were buried at the foot of the orange tree—buried with flowers from every one, and passionate tears from Marie, and many promises, as she kissed the box, not to forget to stop at Paradise for her.

She had not allowed any "grown-ups" to do anything except look on; she and I did all. The mother, wishing to please her, said: "Should we move from here, dear one, we will take up Dinah and keep her with us."

But Marie, with frowning brows, rejected this offer. "No!" she said, "if her now–I–lay–me part got lost out of Paradise, she could come right here and find her old self in her home. If the box was moved, she would be lost everywhere!"

And she went back alone, and I looked and saw her pat the grave gently, and heard her say: "My peshous Dinah!"

Life's Aftermath

Life's Aftermath

"*The grave of all things hath its violet.*"

It was in mellow, many-hued October. It was a Sunday—sunny and still. There was the *feel* of Sunday in the air. Three years had passed since the Great Soldier's prayer, "Let us have peace!" had been answered with blessèd acquiescence. But when, for any reason, the people came together in a crowd, it was sad to see how many still wore mourning. And when the wearer was old or middle-aged, there was something in the deadly composure of manner that said as plain as words: "This will be my garb as long as life shall last!"

One woman there was who watched with envious eye those who passed her wearing "deep mourning." Envious, because she was herself denied the sad satisfaction of this outward expression of her great grief. Her husband—her dearer self—had simply abhorred the custom—the "social bondage," as he called it—of mourning! The wrapping up of the strained and shaken body in black garments, and then the shutting out of every breath of pure air, every ray of God's sunlight with yards on yards of the most hideous product of the manufacturing world—black *crêpe*—was, he declared, detrimental to good health when worn willingly, and when worn *unwillingly*, it was hypocrisy as vulgar as it was cruel. And he had exacted a solemn promise from her, that in the approaching hour of her loss, she would wear no *crêpe* at all, and black only for the briefest possible time; a concession made to save her from the wondering and satirical comments of her friends and neighbors.

Now suddenly the church bells, the chimes, burst forth and tossed high their ringing notes into the pellucid air, sweet reminders to the Great-All Father that His children, sinning, bewildered, yet loving, trusting still, were gathering from afar to kneel and humbly pray together; remembering well those words big with promise: "When two or three are gathered together in my name!"

And among the moving multitude, two women from opposite sides of the city were approaching the same church. Both were middle-aged, and both felt that, in the better sense, their lives were over. Both were victims of the war; both had lost their nearest and dearest; and one, her home as well. And now, among strangers, she wore her rusty *crêpe* with a dignified, almost haughty carriage of body, which, nevertheless, said plainly: "Here is the poverty which is so cruel to the well-bred and refined!" She worked to eke out her small pittance of an income, but there was no sweetness, no savor in her work. She knew she was growing hard and bitter in her sorrow and loneliness, but what did it matter now; there was no dear one to be wounded by her sarcastic speech. "A childless widow!" she murmured, "why do I encumber the earth? There is no living thing that needs me, that is glad of my coming," and she shuddered in her thin, black garments as she thought of the years that, dull and cold, might be waiting her, and then saw the church, and tried to bring her thoughts under control.

The other woman (she who sighed to wear black), moving slowly and heavily, wondered why neither the bright, warm sun nor the heavy, handsome camel's-hair shawl in which, to the surprise of her neighbors, she was closely wrapped this warm day, could conquer that little, creeping chill in her blood that every now and then developed into a shiver. But she gave that matter scant thought. Weary and dull to her, the very bells seemed to ring out over and over again the one word, "A-lone! A-lone!"

She had her comfortable, even handsome, home; ample means to keep it up, but it was so empty! There was no one to watch for, to dress for, to plan for, cook for! No one to give her greeting, or loving thanks for loving service. She was utterly alone, and she was only forty-four, and might live—good God! how long? If it were not unlawful so to do, she would kneel here in the church she was entering and pray to die at once, that she might fill her appointed place between her husband and her son, and be at rest.

With such thoughts, these women approached the church and each other. Foolish, wicked thoughts, you say. Perhaps, but for a woman who is growing old; whose heart is bleeding from many wounds, it is so hard a thing to face the great world alone. But so it came about that as Mrs. Martha Swift, of Ohio, sat in pew 71, an usher waved into pew 72 Mrs. Marion Wallace, of Georgia, who was no sooner comfortably seated than a quick shiver shaking the shoulders of the woman in front of her drew her attention to the shoulders and to the shawl about them. And then an odd thing happened. Her glance, at first a merely casual one, had quickly intensified into a prolonged and piercing stare. Then she had raised her veil and studied the shawl as if it had been the horoscope of one she loved; studied it until from the seeming confusion of the innumerable morsels of rich, dim colors tossed together, there came order and a clear design. Then, to the wonderment of two or three observers, she drew off her glove and, leaning forward, passed her bare forefinger eagerly along the edge of that bit of solid color always found in the centre of these precious shawls; did it carefully, as does a woman who searches for some faint stain or mark, and suddenly the blood rushed to her face; she drew back swiftly into her place, resumed her glove, but from "Dearly Beloved," clear through to "Let Your Light so Shine," she never took her eyes from that shawl in front of her.

As Mrs. Swift passed out of church, she thought herself rather unnecessarily crowded by a tall woman in black. She answered two or three friendly comments on her bundled-up appearance by saying that, "heavy shawl and all, she was still cold, at least part of the time," and, "yes, come to think of it, she was shivering half her time yesterday"; "yes, it was a lovely day," and so slipped away as quickly as she could, and started to walk across the Public Square, that she might be alone; and then a woman in black was at her side—a woman whose eyes were big and bright with anger; whose trembling finger tapped her on the arm, as she swiftly said: "Madam, this shawl is not your property; it is mine!"

Mrs. Swift was so startled—so utterly taken aback—that at first she could only stare at the stranger and say, stupidly: "What—what did you say?"

And the stranger, in increasing anger, repeated: "This shawl is not your property—it is mine, I tell you! My most precious treasure—*mine*—and I can prove it, too, by marks you cannot gainsay!"

But Mrs. Swift drew away from the tapping finger, exclaiming: "Do you know who you are talking to? You must be crazy! Why, I've owned this shawl these five years!"

"Five years?" scornfully cried the other, "I owned it long enough to know its full design—the dealer's private mark—that my boy showed me when he brought it to me from his first trip abroad—and in the corner, here on the under side, beneath a rough seam in the border, you will find two letters worked in white silk—an "M" and a "W," and beneath them both a tiny star in many-colored threads. See, then—" She caught swiftly at the corner of the shawl nearest her—turned it back—scanned it closely, and then triumphantly pointed out two small, imperfect letters in white silk—" M " and " W," with the star beneath, as she had said.

Mrs. Swift felt her face flush, but she bravely looked the excited woman in the face : " I do not understand," she said. " This shawl was a gift to me from my only son ! "

" A poor gift that—of ill-gotten property ! " cried the woman in black, and then Martha Swift lifted stern, blue eyes and said : " Madam, my son was a soldier ! He lies out there, beneath his tombstone now ! Do not insult his memory ! "

And she of the black, burning eyes said quickly: " My son fell at the Bloody Angle—he was not identified—and fills some corner of a trench that is marked, if marked at all, by a stone bearing the cruel word, " Unknown !" I insult the memory of no soldier, and I pray you pardon me ! "

Then, all suddenly, they stood with working faces, holding hard to one another's hands, while their tears ran swiftly. They were too deeply moved to speak much then, and they drew down their veils that they might not attract attention.

They had exchanged names and addresses, then walked silently as far as the monument in the centre of the Square. As they were about to separate, Mrs. Swift said: "Mrs. Wallace, this dear shawl is yours, beyond the shadow of a doubt—and back it goes to you, be sure of that—but won't you come to my house, in a day or two, and tell me its story?" Then, seeing refusal dawning on the other's face, she quickly added, "I would so like to hear about your boy!"

Ah, subtle tempter! What mother could resist such sweet flattery! Not this one, who for two long years had not named aloud that beloved son—who entering the army as an elegant young *beau*, had died in broken shoes and tattered clothing—fighting like a demoniac!

Yes, she would come, and Mrs. Swift would tell her side of the story too—would she not? And then it would all come clear between them about the shawl— and there would be blame to no one but herself, perhaps, for her too hasty speech!

And with these promises they parted—each thinking compassionately of the other: "How she must suffer, it is so terrible a thing to lose husband and child too!"

The following Tuesday, on starting out to make the promised visit, Mrs. Wallace became conscious of a lightness, an alertness of movement—of a genuine feeling of interest in the approaching interview, as pleasant as unusual to her. And she wondered a little that she felt in her heart no enmity for this Northern woman who had, beyond a doubt, done her small best to help conquer the South and destroy the beloved "Cause"! But, considered simply as individuals, they were both conquered—beaten—broken down forever! In tastes, up-bringing and experience, they were as far

apart as the poles, but between those two great cries of
motherhood—one wrung from the body's anguish at the
man-child's birth, and the other from the soul's anguish
at his death—the women understood and sympathized
passionately with each other! With these thoughts in
her mind, Mrs. Wallace made her way to the pretty
house, with its bit of lawn, choice shrubs and late
flowers, that belonged to Mrs. Swift, and had the door,
after some delay, thrown open for her by an elderly and
very angry gentleman—evidently a doctor—who continued an unequal contest with two hysterical and belligerent maidens from the " Old Isle "—one of whom,
with the maddening iteration peculiar to her class,
repeated again and again: " 'Twas meself that heard
it!—the Banshee! Bad 'cess to yees—'twas meself that
heard it—the Banshee!—the Banshee!" while the
other, with maudlin tears, vowed she'd " lave that minute
for she couldn't stand hearin' talkin' of blood and—
shootin' and such-like things—besides, when a woman
was crazy, she might kill the lot of them—and such
rucktions she couldn't stand at all—at all! and lave she
must and would!"

Then the doctor locked the door, put the key in his
pocket, and turning to the astonished looker-on, said:
"Let us get out of this hul-a-ba-loo! Come in here,
please, where we can escape from that infernal Banshee!
Now, Madam, Mrs. Swift is a very sick woman!" ("Oh,"
thought Mrs. Wallace, " here is the meaning of those
shiverings, last Sunday!") " She is going to be worse

before she's better; she is absolutely alone save for these rattle-brained servants, who were bad enough to begin with, but are for leaving the poor soul here alone because she has been a bit delirious. You look like a sensible woman and a kind one. Are you an old friend, and can you by chance help her and me now, in this emergency?" Remember, you could not "push the button" then, and let the trained nurse do the rest. There was no button to push, and no trained nurse to answer it. Each family had to care for its own sick. To go to the hospital was looked upon as a degradation. Such nurses as could be had were mostly poor, old, homeless bodies, as ignorant as they were disobedient, and Mrs. Swift's case was not a very uncommon one.

Mrs. Marion Wallace paused—before she answered. She literally could not say, "I am a stranger." At her first slow words, "I am not an *old* friend," such a look of despair came into the doctor's face that she hurriedly added, "but still a friend, and—," slowly removing her bonnet and shawl, she stepped to the hall, took the Banshee's white apron from her, tied it about her own waist, sent the Banshee herself up stairs for a pair of slippers—"anyone's would do"—and returning to the parlor, said, quietly: "Now, Doctor, if you will kindly give me your first instructions in writing, please. You see, I shall have to get this demoralized household set right again. When all is going smoothly, I shall only need to be told your wishes, but just at first—"

And the doctor had stared a moment, and then he

had caught her hands and shook them half off, crying: " You'll stay — you'll take charge here? You're a mighty fine woman, I can tell you that — and what I call a good Christian, by—!" And so this strange, Southern woman came to nurse faithfully her Northern sister in sorrow — to guide her household into ways of clocklike regularity, and so heard the story of the shawl, not once, but many times—but always told with fever-cracked lips—with burning eyes and hands wandering and restless, and alas, always with hoarse entreaties to believe her — her boy could not steal — no, not even for her, his mother! He had bought the shawl from one who swore he had come by it honestly! If only the strange woman with the angry eyes would believe her! "You see, it came about like this"—she would say, and wearily begin all over again, to explain —to convince—to defend!

Then one day the subject of her rambling talk was changed. She seemed to be reading some account of a Northern victory — over and over again, she repeated all the details — the calmness of the great General — the wild delight of the victorious troops!—the rags and hunger of the prisoners—and always ended with: "The enemy lost two thousand men killed and five thousand wounded!"

Mrs. Wallace had listened to the harassing repetition of this Northern triumph until her strained nerves could bear no more, and was turning with a flushed face to leave the bedside, when a sort of gasping sob stopped her. Once more the sick woman repeated: "The enemy lost two thousand men killed—" and then, in a tone lowered almost to a whisper, she added: "Oh, the wives and the mothers!—two thousand killed! Oh, dear God, be merciful to the poor mothers — the heart-broken mothers of the South!" and Mrs. Wallace sank upon her knees, and taking the burning hand of the sick woman in her own, she cried: "Great heart! I will love you all my life, for that gentle prayer!"

The words seemed to reach the inner counsciousness of the sufferer— her hot, blue eyes turned their glance upon the calm, brown ones beside her, where they wavered for a moment — steadied — rested, and then recognition dawned in them, and a weak voice whispered: " You said—?"

"I said I loved you for your great heart!" answered Mrs. Wallace.

A faint brightness came to the sick face, and she said: "Then don't leave me ever! We can love and mourn our dead together! Life is so hard — to bear alone—be my sister—Marion!"

They looked long into each other's eyes. They must have thought of many things! But it was as if the hands of their dear, dead boys drew them together. And Mrs. Wallace gently answered: "I will not leave you while you want me, Martha! We will walk together, if you will it, till we are called to join our dear ones;" their hands met in a close clasp, and in ten minutes Mrs. Swift was asleep. After Mrs. Swift had recovered, the neighbors spent all their spare time, and a good deal that was not spare, in wondering "when that Southern woman was going away?"

Early in the winter they had seen two trunks and a large picture brought to the house, but they watched in vain for the exit of the aforesaid two trunks and picture. What could it mean? They all declared Mrs. Swift too active a woman to want a housekeeper—too strong to need a nurse — too proud and too well off to have a boarder! But surely she would have to go soon, now that spring was almost upon them! And lo! one sunny spring morning, both ladies, with garden hats firmly tied on, and loose old gloves protecting their hands, were out in the garden, making life a misery and bewilderment to the harmless, nearly useless old gardener, who, doddering about, accepted their orders with a respectful misunderstanding of them that promised rare developments for the future. One thing they did, though, with their own hands. Mrs. Swift had obtained a fine, young magnolia—a gift for Mrs. Wallace. It was a pretty thought, and Mrs. Wallace accepted shrub and thought with warm gratitude. And together, with smiles, and may be a tear or two, they planted the magnolia on the lawn, and at the same time filled the souls of the neighbors with a very anguish of curiosity.

When summer came, notes from a well-played piano floated from the open windows of Mrs. Swift's house, and no matter what classic composition Mrs. Wallace might begin with, she always closed her playing with

"In the Hazel Dell," because that had been the favorite song of the young Northern soldier, and his mother loved to hear the simple, old air for his dear sake.

Winter came, and the two trunks and the picture had not been removed. The neighbors had fallen into a sort of torpor. Then, one day, one rushed to the others, declaring: "They call each other by their first names! Yes, Mrs. Swift said: 'Marion, there must be double windows for your room this winter!' and that Southern woman answers up: 'Oh, no, Martha, that's not necessary!' What do you think of that?" Evidently there was no use in watching the house, after that, for the departure of the Southern woman.

During the long winter evenings, this elderly couple used to talk unceasingly of the war, and they would tell one another of this or that engagement, illustrating the positions of the troops with spools of thread, the scissors always coming handy for streams that had to be crossed. Then Mrs. Swift never tired of hearing what the war had meant to the women of the South. She wept over the burned houses, the looted property, the hunger, the make-shift for clothing, and would draw her rocker closer to Mrs. Wallace, as she told how the last precious ounces of real coffee had been hidden—as people hide gold or jewels—only to be brought forth in tiny portions for a sick or wounded soldier—told how she had cut up old garments of her husband's to make herself shoes, and had worn skirts made from her sitting-room curtains!

When spring came again, and Decoration Day arrived, Mrs. Wallace felt that Mrs. Swift, for the first time, showed a lack of tact—of proper feeling—in insisting upon having her accompany her to the cemetery that day. It would be very painful to see the graves, all flower-covered, and to think of her own dear, unhonored dead, lying so far away. This insistence was so unlike Mrs. Swift's usual manner, too! Well, she must bear it! and so she entered the carriage, with a heavy heart, to drive to the cemetery, and wondered a little why Mrs. Swift had two great wreaths, instead of one, to lay upon the grave.

When they arrived, she wished to remain in the carriage, but again Mrs. Swift insisted upon having her company, and together they made their way to the family plot, and there stood the explanation of Mrs. Swift's strange conduct—a fair, white stone, bearing the name of Wallace instead of Swift. And Mrs. Wallace knelt humbly down to read that this monument was in memory of the young captain, Marion Wallace, whose body lay in the distant State where he had fallen fighting for the "cause" he loved! As she pressed her lips upon the name on the stone, she solemnly vowed that the welfare of the woman who had done this thing should be the one object of her life hereafter.

And so they faced the world together. A gentle pair, helping the poor or the troubled; trusting and admiring each other; Mrs. Swift honestly believing Mrs. Wallace was the greatest pianist in the city, and that her feeble little sketches were remarkable works of art, while Mrs. Wallace stood in speechless wonder at Mrs. Swift's ability, with only the help of an inch or two of stubby pencil and a morsel of paper, to bring perfect order out of the chaos of her accounts. And though she had something less than three hundred a year, it was really astonishing the muddle she could get her affairs into! So it's no wonder that she respected Mrs. Swift as an mathematician of parts.

The shawl was worn by one as often as the other, though it was acknowledged to be Mrs. Wallace's property, since she owned it for years before that day when young Lieutenant Swift had purchased it from a soldier who declared he had bought it for a few dollars from an old contraband camp-follower. And as they shared the shawl, so they shared everything—duties, pleasures, or personal belongings. Each acted as housekeeper, month about. If one was daintier, the other had more executive ability. They came to understand each other so perfectly that when Mrs. Wallace sometimes sat completely lost in thought, Mrs. Swift could tell, from the expression of her face, whether she was thinking of her son's young manhood and soldierly death or of his baby days when within the tender circle of her arms he found a very tower of defence against the world.

The last time I saw them they were in church—the same church where they first saw each other. Two sweet-faced, old women; one blue-eyed, one dark-eyed, but both with whitened hair, each anxious to serve the other; Mrs. Swift a trifle quicker about wraps and foot-stools, but Mrs. Wallace smilingly ahead in the finding of places in hymnal or prayer book. As they sat with attentive, uplifted faces, I thought they looked like two ancient children who had walked hand in hand over a long, rough road that *alone* either would have shrunk from.

True sympathy had drawn all bitterness from their grief, while their unshakable faith in the resurrection of the body and the Life everlasting, had kept Hope alive in their souls! Hope for that " Life of the world to come "! And Hope's sweetness was in their old eyes and about their paled, tremulous lips, as they worshipped there.

The last prayer said, each instinctively put out her hand to assist the other to rise. Their hands met; so did their eyes, and they smiled at each other, and at that very moment the sunlight, striking on the stained-glass window, flung a very halo of splendid color about their dear, white heads, the church thus smiling upon them as they smiled upon each other; and I said to myself: "The Aftermath—truly they have garnered their Life's Aftermath!"

www.ingramcontent.com/pod-product-compliance
Lightning Source LLC
Chambersburg PA
CBHW022056230426
43672CB00008B/1185